GOD'S PASSIN

A MANUAL ON CHURCH PLANTING

FOR WORLD EVANGELISM

BUD CALVERT

Striving Together Publications
4020 E. Lancaster Blvd.
Lancaster, CA 93535
800.201.7748

Cover design by Andrew Jones
Layout by Craig Parker and Beth Lee
Edited by Tina Butterfield
Special thanks to our proofreaders.

ISBN 978-1-59894-115-9

Printed in the United States of America

DEDICATION

In 1 Thessalonians 3:2, Paul called Timothy a *"brother, and minister of God, and our fellowlabourer in the gospel of Christ...."* How I thank God for the many brothers, sisters, and fellow laborers I have had in the Gospel ministry at the Fairfax Baptist Temple. Beside the many staff, deacons, and other faithful workers of our church, the ones who have made this book possible because of their examples and distinguished service are the thirty-four men listed below, who have been commissioned by our church to start a church and two who have taken over existing churches. When counting the number of churches that all these men have started out of their churches, along with ours, the number is seventy-five and counting!

I dedicate this book to our church planters:

Todd Abbey	Jeff Berg	Matt Walker
David Hosaflook	Terry McGuire	Tony Ghareeb
Dick Abbot	Troy Calvert	Scott Wendal
Rich Hurst	Paul Stalnecker	Rick Goette
Mike Aylestock	Marc Deloach	Ken Wheelock
Jeff Kelly	Jack Ramos	Gil Hansen III
Sam Aylestock	Phil Phillips	Tim York
Jim Kiefer	Bill DeWeese	Andrew Henderson
Lou Baldwin	Daniel Pigott	Joshua Zuray
Kye Kim	Kyle Fannin	Areobaldo DeCarvalho
Gary Bell	David Pigott	
Mike Leczo	Lynn Floth	

CONTENTS

ACKNOWLEDGMENTS

I owe a great debt of gratitude to Dr. Ted Wieler for his patient and faithful editing help with this book. Dr. Wieler, an attorney and staff member at Fairfax Baptist Temple, has been very gracious with his time and input. He has very meticulously gone over the manuscript and made invaluable suggestions and helpful notations. Without his help, this book would not be in your hands.

I would also like to thank Mary, my wife, for supporting me these forty years in the ministry. She has been not only my faithful and caring wife but also my greatest encourager, always supporting me in every aspect of ministering through the years. My thanks to her, also, for proofreading this book. God is good!

The people of the Fairfax Baptist Temple are always on my heart, and I thank them for allowing me to be their pastor for thirty-five years. I believe it is their example that has been the paradigm for the many church planters who have been commissioned by our church.

FOREWORD

from Dr. Paul Chappell

As I drive up our western coast and pass city after city with no Gospel-preaching, soulwinning church, I'm burdened. All throughout our nation and around the world there are cities, towns, and villages where no one has yet answered God's call to plant a church.

The book you hold is about correcting this problem. It is about understanding God's passion for church planting and world evangelism, and then syncing our heartbeat to His.

Since the earliest days of the New Testament church, God has given local churches the responsibility to be witnesses *"both in Jerusalem, and in all Judaea, and in Samaria, and unto the uttermost part of the earth"* (Acts 1:8). Even as we witness for Christ in our respective "Jerusalems," He intends that we reach beyond by planting other churches—in nearby towns and all the way to the uttermost part of the earth. This is God's passion and plan for world evangelism.

Church planting is more than close to God's heart—it is His very pulse. Christ loved the church so much that He gave Himself for it (Ephesians 5:25). But too often, we make the business of reproducing other churches a peripheral matter.

It has been my joy over the past few years to witness a renewed fervor among independent Baptists for church planting. God is raising up courageous men who understand His passion. Like the prophet Isaiah, they have heard the Lord call *"Whom shall I send,"* and they have willingly offered *"Here am I; send me"* (Isaiah 6:8).

My friend, Dr. Bud Calvert, is such a man. Wholly applying himself to the task of church planting, God has used Dr. Calvert to also awake a heart for God's passion in scores of men. Many of these have become church planters. Others are pastors who have understood the need to send church planters. Still others are laypeople who now invest their energy, through prayer, soulwinning, and financial support, into new church plants.

I'm thankful Dr. Calvert has written this book. Not only does it contain a rich mine of truth and practical help for church planting, but I pray it will reignite the hearts of God's people to God's passion of church planting for world evangelization.

Paul Chappell
Lancaster, California
September 2010

INTRODUCTION

Throughout this book, I have written descriptively of what I learned and practiced during the thirty-five years I was the pastor of Fairfax Baptist Temple. While I am not presently the pastor—the church voted to have my son take on the responsibilities of that office—I decided that writing to you as one standing where you presently stand and walking where you presently walk, makes for an easier conversation.

I am writing this book because I believe that churches planting churches is God's plan for evangelizing the world. In the early section of the book, I take just a few pages to explain from the Bible why churches are to plant churches. The greatest bulk of the book is a discussion of how a church goes about the work of church planting. That is the area in which pastors tell me they need the most help. Most of the men holding the office are aware of God's emphasis on church planting, but they are not certain that they know how to accomplish it. The place to start is on your knees.

Knowing everything there is to know in the Bible about the *why* of church planting and knowing exactly how to enter a community and start a church is not of much value if there is no one from your congregation who responds to the call of God to go do it. Inherent in what I just said is my belief that there are very few congregations where God has not tried to call men and boys to be church planters. I do not believe the problem is God's silence; I believe the problem is a deafness to the call or an unwillingness to respond. If you start praying and faithfully continue that prayer day after day, if you start talking about church planting from the pulpit and in casual conversation because it is foremost on your heart, if you start setting aside funds in your church budget against the day you are ready to commission and send off church planters, you may be surprised just how quickly one man after another starts wondering aloud to you whether God just might be calling. When they do, your duty is clear. You must do whatever you can to prepare those men to go. It is in preparation for that day—a day that will be a highlight in your ministry life—that I have written this book.

You will want to have on hand a resource for helping these God-chosen men. The focus of this discussion is decidedly on church planting in the United States though many of the principles are equally valid for the missionary-evangelist on the foreign field. It may, in fact, be easier for the missionary in Uganda to negotiate for land with the head of the clan in a village than it is for a church planter to ask the school board in New York to allow him to meet in one of their buildings!

What you will be reading has been field tested. The process works, though every church plant is in some way unique. I love reading the story that begins in Acts 11:25 *"Then departed Barnabas to Tarsus, for to seek Saul"* and continues in Acts 13:1–2:

> *Now there were in the church that was at Antioch certain prophets and teachers; as Barnabas, and Simeon that was called Niger, and Lucius of Cyrene, and Manaen, which had been brought up with Herod the tetrarch, and Saul. As they ministered to the Lord, and fasted, the Holy Ghost said, Separate me Barnabas and Saul for the work whereunto I have called them.*

Remember, in Matthew when Jesus saw the multitudes with no shepherd, he didn't worry or respond as though there were no hope. At that point, the Bible gave the clear-cut answer for the shortage of workers: *"Then saith he unto his disciples, the harvest truly is plenteous, but the labourers are few; pray ye therefore the lord of the harvest, that he will send forth labourers into his harvest"* (Matthew 9:37–38).

Pastor, there is a man in your church that needs you to be his Barnabas. Saul (Paul) needed to be encouraged to engage himself in the work God had called him to do. Saul needed Barnabas to seek him, to encourage him, and to train him, just as the men in your congregation need you.

There is a world full of people that are hungry to know the Bread of Life. *"How then shall they call on him in whom they have not believed? and how shall they believe in him of whom they have not heard? and how shall they hear without a preacher? And how shall they preach, except they be sent?"* (Romans 10:14–15).

If you are a man studying and praying about whether God would have you leave your home church and plant a new church, I want you to know that I am praying for you in just the same way our great God and Saviour prayed for our salvation in John 17:20. I don't know you and may never meet you, but because I am praying that God would send more laborers to the harvest, I've been praying for you for over forty years.

You are probably a little apprehensive as you look to your future as a pastor or missionary-evangelist. Just thinking about going to a place where you know no one, or perhaps only a few, to begin the process of changing lives is a daunting thought. How do you get a group of strangers to change their Sunday morning and evening habits, their Wednesday evening habits, their weekday and weekend routines to voluntarily come and sit in a not-so-comfortable chair for an hour or two to hear you talk about a Book that they probably have never read, with the goal of having these strangers trust their eternity to a God they have never personally embraced? Just try to tell me that you are not about to embark on a supernatural journey! All of this would be borderline crazy were it not for the fact that it is God who has called you to do it. Keep that in mind. Any "success" you have is God's and His alone.

I have written this book to help you in much the same way I would help you if you were one of my own church planting interns. This is a resource to help keep your efforts focused in the right direction as you plan your church planting campaign. As you will find from reading this book, the plan is for you to work in close association with your pastor. Listen to him. Learn from him. Take what he says to you and give it a fair chance to work. He will expect that you will have to make some modifications along the way. But, it is foolhardy and wasteful to insist on inventing everything on your own. Ask him what has worked and what has not worked over the years. Draw out of him his thoughts concerning why some things went as he had hoped and others did not. The counsel of Proverbs 20:5 could not be more appropriate. *"Counsel in the heart of man is like deep water; but a man of understanding will draw it out."*

ANY "SUCCESS" YOU HAVE IS GOD'S AND HIS ALONE.

It is possible that your pastor has never sent out a man to plant a church. He may not have been a church planter himself, but I will tell you with certainty that he still has a wealth of ideas and hours of study in the Word of God that I know the Spirit will use to accomplish what the Bible declares to be His purpose and plan.

You will also want to stay in close contact with your pastor. The number of situations that will jump out in front of you are too numerous to mention. Every day you will be faced with problems that right now you cannot even imagine (and shouldn't try to imagine!). When that happens, bring to bear all of the wisdom that God has given you, pray earnestly, and don't forget that your pastor has probably walked the road you are now traveling and can help.

So, gentlemen, sending pastor and church planter alike, grab your Sword, put on your Shield, shod your feet, and walk boldly into the white harvest field.

A final word to the "layman" that may be reading this book out of a desire to be actively engaged in the work of church planting world evangelism. Thank you for your interest! Precious little of the work in the local church ministry is accomplished by the pastor or his paid staff. Much of the heavy lifting is done by you. You have a large part to play as your church sends out families to plant new churches. And, who knows, perhaps by the time you finish reading this book, you will realize that your interest was just one more indication that God is speaking to your heart about His best for your life. That, at least, is my prayer.

ONE

THE HEART
OF THE GREAT COMMISSION

*Go ye therefore, and teach all nations, baptizing them in
the name of the Father, and of the Son, and of the Holy
Ghost: Teaching them to observe all things whatsoever I have
commanded you: and, lo, I am with you always, even unto
the end of the world.*—MATTHEW 28:19–20

We might ask ourselves, "Why church planting?
What's the big deal about starting churches?
Everyone knows that the local church has been
given the Great Commission, so what's the fuss? Why have this
fervency of heart for the Great Commission?"

Often young men graduate from Bible college and are
challenged to go immediately to start a church. First on their
agenda (they are told) is to think through and then write
down a memorable phrase that tells people what the primary
distinctive of their church will be. Then the drill is to write a
short but inclusive statement that succinctly gives the members
of the new church an easily memorized statement to focus their
attention on the task at hand. In doing so, everyone will work

1

off the same page and know what it is they want to accomplish. After all, if a young pastor cannot clearly define his objective, how will he ever know if he succeeds in reaching it? That sounds like a reasonable challenge to a young pastor, so he does his best to put his church on the map as some innovative, state-of-the-art, up-to-date assembly that is going some place!

While the exercise has value, I suggest to any young preacher starting out that he should first spend some serious time meditating on what Jesus Christ told the fledging first century church He wanted their focus to be. Jesus Christ died and shed His blood to further a plan established before the world began. Our Lord left us here with a clear compass to direct His church. The succinct statement the young pastor writes must find itself in the statement made by the Head of the church, a statement clearly set out in Matthew 28:19–20, Mark 16:15, Luke 24:46–47, and Acts 1:8. Jesus made it very clear so that neither I nor any other pastor has to wonder what is the overarching goal we are all to try to achieve. It is important, though, that every pastor thinks through *how* he his going to lead his church to carry out that commission.

The purpose of the church is clearly spelled out in the Great Commission. The desperate need of the day is for churches to embrace that God-given purpose, and then to articulate a plan for *accomplishing* His purpose. Many have never properly understood that the Great Commission defines the work of the

OUR LORD LEFT US HERE WITH A CLEAR COMPASS TO DIRECT HIS CHURCH.

local church. It's simple because it's in the Bible, but many have never taken it to heart. I doubt there is a true church in existence today that doesn't know that the responsibility to carry out the Great Commission is ours. But what is missing is the *passion* to carry it out!

I think sometimes we pastors can get too caught up in the minutiae of what is expected in a good pastor. The distraction of good things—yea, even necessary things—just keeps snowballing. Everyday we need to think, "To whom can I give this? What else can be delegated?" There is so much to be done all the time, but we should never get so caught up in the details that we forget our priority.

There's nothing that thrills me more than those who get out and start churches. They have a hunger and a zeal for reaching people. It is easy for some of you who have been in the pastorate for a while to reminisce about getting out there, knocking on doors, and passing out tracts or door hangers and think, "Ah, those were the good old days," those days before you had all the other ministries going and all the additional responsibilities that have developed along the way. Somehow, you've become an administrator, a financier, an educator, a contractor, a counselor, and a million other things. I'm here to tell you that *these* are the good old days! To rekindle the flame, you just get out and knock on doors, win people to Christ, and preach the Word of God.

We need passion for what we are doing! We easily become satisfied and develop an attitude of "we four and no more." Maybe you and your people are satisfied with the status quo, the "if they're happy with me, I'm happy with them" mentality. If that is where you are in ministry, you need to change! The goal of reaching our world for Christ through church planting needs to move from being a program of the church to the passion of the pastor and the entire church.

World evangelism should be the heartbeat of the church. Too often, however, it is relegated to an annual conference, and even that is conducted half-heartedly. Unfortunately, some pastors view this conference as a disruption to the "real work" of their local church ministry and try to get through it as quickly as possible. But churches after God's passion live with the task of world evangelism always before them. They understand that it is their mission and their purpose.

Why does there seem to be so little passion for world evangelism? I know one thing that will light a fire in any missions conference—sending out one of your own young men to start a church or one of your own men or young ladies to labor on the foreign mission field. Commissioning your own will make missions very personal to the church.

My guess is that 90 percent of all churches have never started a church out of their church—*on purpose*, that is. Many churches have succumbed to splits, but I don't mean starting a church that way; I mean starting more churches *on purpose*. Church planting is at the heart of the Great Commission and should be in the heart of every single church.

Every church is known for something: music program, youth meetings, preaching, building size, school, or any number of different things. Why not be known for your church planting program? Why not just say, "*This* is what is vital to the work of the ministry, so *this* is what I must do"? It is simply a matter of priorities. You must have the priority in its proper place. You must say, "This is what I want. This is what's important—starting churches." When you start a church, whether anyone else knows your labor and sacrifice, God sees you as a pastor who is faithful to the task.

CHURCH PLANTING IS AT THE HEART OF THE GREAT COMMISSION.

I read about a fellow who was driving his fancy car around a turn on a mountain in West Virginia. Because he was going a little bit too fast around the curve, he went over the guardrail and the car went tumbling down the slope. Fortunately, there was somebody right behind him. He stopped his car, jumped out, and ran down the hill. There he found the driver crying out, "Oh, my Mercedes, my Mercedes, my Mercedes!" That's all he could think about.

The other guy said, "Sir, it's worse than that. I hate to tell you, but your left arm is severed as well."

"Oh, my Rolex, my Rolex, my Rolex!"

It's a matter of values and priorities. We have to think about what is important in our churches. It's not our buildings. It's not our youth programs. It's not our senior citizens programs. Our priorities should be centered on evangelizing this world that we might best glorify God. All of these other things help in the ministry, but we are to give ourselves completely to God and to the work of world evangelism.

WHAT THE GREAT COMMISSION IS NOT

Let's think for a few moments about the things that churches get involved in that are not fulfilling the purpose Jesus set before us.

The Great Commission is not philanthropy. It is not benevolence. My guess is that philanthropy and benevolence would be involved in the answer that most mainline denominations would give if asked to define their purpose. Our churches, of course, are not hospitals or jail ministries or homeless shelters. They're not battered women's shelters or orphanages. While all of these things are good and can be tools to reach people with the Gospel, they are not in and of themselves fulfilling the Great Commission. Many churches are turning to social programs as a substitute for the real thing. We must make Christ's last command our first priority.

Our missions programs should strictly be used to obey the Great Commission. They should not have anything in them that would directly benefit our churches. We don't use missions money to support our own local church ministries. While soulwinning is often involved in these ministries, missions and world evangelism take place outside the doors of the local church. We don't put these other items in our church missions budget. We set aside and use missions dollars for starting churches and planting churches—stateside or overseas—through our own missionary-evangelists and those sent out from other like-minded churches. We never do anything with the missions funds unless it is to benefit someone away from the work of our local church. Our missions programs are to be beyond the scope of our local church.

A BETTER UNDERSTANDING OF MATTHEW 28

Our churches, clearly, have the responsibility to go into all the world and preach the Gospel. To my preacher brethren: I know you have studied and preached this passage as much as I have. However, please allow me to refresh your memory on some of its aspects and perhaps instruct others who are not as familiar with the passage as you are. I am laying a foundation for what is to follow. So, with that explanation, let us mind God's instruction through a little exegetical study of these verses to enable us to get a more thorough understanding of our God and Saviour's commission to His church.

> *Go ye therefore, and teach all nations, baptizing them in the name of the Father, and of the Son, and of the Holy Ghost: Teaching them to observe all things whatsoever I have commanded you: and, lo, I am with you always, even unto the end of the world.*—Matthew 28:19–20

Let's start with the phrase *"teach all nations."* The word used here for *teach* is *matheteuo*. Its definition is entirely different than the modern meaning of *teach* because it literally means "to make disciples." This is the heart and command of the Great Commission. *"Go ye therefore and teach"* or make disciples of all people. So, I want to give out the Word of God; I want to make disciples.

To make disciples of people is to lead them to a saving knowledge of the Teacher, the Lord Jesus Christ. It is to get others to become what we are, if you will.

Look at the scope of our teaching. We are to *"teach **all** nations"* the Bible says (emphasis added). This means that it is incumbent upon every pastor and every church to broaden their vision on ministering to the whole world. It should be an easy matter to count the countries of the world, but it is not. The U.S. State Department's official list of independent countries is 194. As I read the list, however, I discovered a footnote that says, for political reasons, Taiwan is not counted even though it meets all the criteria. So, I thought 195 was the correct answer. I read further, learning that there are more than 60 territories, colonies, and dependencies—places governed by another country. These include regions like Puerto Rico, Greenland, and the components of the United Kingdom. This means that there are about 255 places on the earth that have names and territorial limits, 255 places to send missionaries with the Good News that salvation by grace through faith in Jesus Christ is available to all who will believe.

> IT IS INCUMBENT UPON EVERY PASTOR AND EVERY CHURCH TO BROADEN THEIR VISION ON MINISTERING TO THE WHOLE WORLD.

Nations, in Matthew 28:19–20, is a translation of the Greek word, *ethnos*, from which we get our English word *ethnic*. In other words, not only is it our responsibility to go into all the 255 countries in the world, but it is also our responsibility to evangelize every ethnic group in the world. It is said that there are some 16,469 ethnic or people groups in the world and that there are 6,859 unreached ethnic groups in the world, most of which are in the 10/40 window.

One might say, "It is impossible for one church to involve itself in evangelism of such an enormous scope. We will never get churches planted everywhere." My response has always been, "Our church will have more fun trying than their church will not trying!"

Notice when we are to do this. The Bible says, "**Go.**" The word *go* literally means "going" or "while you are going." That's the whole thought behind the word *go*. As you are going, you are to make disciples of all nations.

In other words, it is assumed that the Christians in our churches will be interacting with society and sometimes even taking trips to foreign places. "While I am going" is the whole idea. While I am going, I am to be giving out tracts; I am to be talking to people about the Lord. While I am going I am to be witnessing to others; I am to be reaching more people for Jesus Christ, with the ultimate goal of starting more churches. What a joy and a privilege evangelism really is!

Some time ago, I went to an Exxon station to see if I could get a quick oil change. I saw one of the employees and asked, "Sir, do you have a good price on an oil change?"

He said, "Yes, we do, $19.95."

"That sounds like a good price," I said. "Any chance you could take me right now?" (I had plenty of time, but, you know, we're always in a hurry!)

He went to check and soon returned. "Yes, we can," he said.

As I reached into my pocket to get a tract, I said, "Here's a tract I'd like to give you that will tell you how you can go to Heaven."

"I thought you looked familiar," he said. "You're Pastor Calvert, aren't you?" Then he proceeded to tell me that he and his wife had visited the Fairfax Baptist Temple about twenty years before, and afterward I came by his house to visit them.

That night both he and his wife accepted the Lord Jesus Christ as their personal Saviour. He then said, "I want you to know that we're still faithful in church—not yours, but another one." (Well, you don't keep them all!)

That same week, two days later, I got a phone call from a man who said, "This is so-and-so. I sold you a car several years ago. Remember me?"

I said, "Yes, I do remember you."

"You gave me a little pamphlet," he said, "and talked to me about the Lord. I've been thinking about you for the last couple of years. On a scale of one to ten, my life is a zero right now. Is there any chance at all that I might be able to talk with you?" The next day he came to my office and got saved!

It's while we are going; it's while we're out there—not just on a Tuesday or Thursday night—but it's while we are going that we are to be teaching all nations and doing what we can for the Lord. From a practical standpoint, it means we should be witnesses at work. In our neighborhoods we should be witnessing as well. Thank God, two or three years ago, I baptized my next-door neighbor—a doctor, who received Christ in our kitchen, and his wife, who accepted Christ a little later. As the psalmist said, "*He that goeth forth and weepeth, bearing precious seed, shall doubtless come again with rejoicing, bringing his sheaves with him"* (Psalm 126:6).

In society at large, we should be on a mission to make disciples of all people. Our attitude ought to be that of the rescue worker on a search and rescue team who leaves no rock unturned. These people turn over every stone in search of victims. They sometimes risk their lives, as they did in New York and Washington on 9/11. They definitely lay aside their personal comforts for the benefit of other people.

The next-door neighbor I just mentioned was the head doctor at the Pentagon on 9/11. He said the rescue team basically lived at a motel close by so they could catch a few hours sleep and then return to the Pentagon to rescue and care for more people. This is the sense of urgency we are all supposed to have. Who knows when any one person will face his eternity?

> WE SHOULD BE ON A MISSION TO MAKE DISCIPLES OF ALL PEOPLE.

The Great Commission has multiple parts to it. We are to make disciples of everyone who will believe. We are then to baptize them, realizing that to dip or immerse them is the first step of obedience after a person has been saved. While talking to a couple in my office recently, I had the joy of leading the man to the Lord. I then turned to the wife who said she had been saved but not baptized. After I shared with them the scriptural command to be baptized, they both came in obedience to Christ that next Sunday and were baptized. We are to keep at it all the time: get them saved and scripturally baptized.

Although this is not a new teaching for most of us, the last responsibility Matthew 28:20 specifies is that we teach these newly saved and baptized disciples to observe everything. In other words, the Great Commission does not stop with someone's salvation. This is where Bible study fellowship classes and preaching services come in. One-on-one discipleship is important for new believers. It should not, however, be done as a replacement for the Sunday school program, and certainly not for the preaching ministry. You can't get any better discipling than you do from the pulpit or in Sunday school programs. New believers and mature believers alike benefit greatly from church-wide worship and Bible study. As we disciple one-on-one, let's not forget the admonition of Hebrews 10:25 to assemble together.

We need to ask ourselves, "To whom was the Great Commission intended?" Was it just for the eleven disciples to whom the words were directly spoken? Of course, we know the answer to that is *no*. If that were true, the Great Commission would have died when the eleven disciples died. Was it given to Christians in general? No, because there were no other Christians present when Jesus gave the commission. I believe it was given to the church. Keep in mind when the church started.

When Jesus came into the coasts of Caesarea Philippi, he asked his disciples, saying, Whom do men say that I the Son of man am? And they said, Some say that thou art John the Baptist: some, Elias; and others, Jeremias, or one of the prophets. He saith unto them, But whom say ye that I am? And Simon Peter answered and said,

Thou art the Christ, the Son of the living God. And Jesus answered and said unto him, Blessed art thou, Simon Barjona: for flesh and blood hath not revealed it unto thee, but my Father which is in heaven. And I say also unto thee, That thou art Peter, and upon this rock I will build my church; and the gates of hell shall not prevail against it.—Matthew 16:13–18

This passage indicates to me that the Lord is letting Peter know that He is beginning His work of building His church. We should keep in mind that Jesus selected the apostles in Luke 6:12 and 13, before He gave the Great Commission. And we know from 1 Corinthians 12:28 that Jesus set the apostles in the church: "*And God hath set some in the church, first apostles, secondarily prophets, thirdly teachers, after that miracles, then gifts of healings, helps, governments, diversities of tongues.*" If the first people put in the church were apostles (selected back in Luke 6), I don't believe He had to wait through all the time that elapsed prior to Acts 1 to start the church. It was at Pentecost that the already existing church, the apostles and other believers, received its energizing and sustaining power—the indwelling Holy Spirit—to perform the Great Commission. What I'm focusing on is this: Jesus commissioned the apostles—those who composed the church at its inception. **It is the church to whom Jesus gave the Great Commission.**

When He commissioned this early church, Jesus said "*…all power is given unto me…*" (Matthew 28:18). The word *power* is a translation of *exousia*, meaning "authority." All "authority" is given unto me. The local church derives all of its authority from the Lord. And it is *only* the church that has the authority to carry out the Great Commission.

Because the Great Commission was given to the church, and because it is performed by believers organized together as a local church, and because there is a limit to the immediate reach of any local body of believers—a limit to how far believers can travel to assemble together regularly—there must be in God's plan a means for populating the earth with churches. The only way this can be done is through church planting—local churches reproducing themselves beyond their own "Jerusalem" to reach Judaea, Samaria, and the uttermost.

> IT IS THE CHURCH TO WHOM JESUS GAVE THE GREAT COMMISSION.

When you hear about someone operating on his own who wins a convert and then baptizes him in a swimming pool somewhere, please understand that is not biblical baptism because he has no biblical authority to baptize. The act of immersion does not constitute biblical baptism. That's part of it to be sure, but the ordinance has to have the right authority (local church) behind it.

The church was given the authority. The local church has the commission. The local church has the power. The local church has the resources. And the local church has the Word of God and the people. We've got it all! We have everything that God wants us to have to do His work.

IT IS THE CHURCH'S COMMISSION

In the discussion that has preceded, I have explained the Great Commission and how it is to be accomplished. Implicit in the discussion is the assumption that the Great Commission is performed by the local church. Sometimes we hear about para-church organizations that are started to accomplish some facet of the Great Commission—supporting a failing church or reaching a particular group of people. While I have no doubt that the people starting these organizations are well intentioned— I'm sure in most cases the people have in their heart a desire to reach people with the Word of God— nothing, however, in the Word of God suggests that the Great Commission is to be performed by any organization other than the local church.

Some will protest: "But for the work of this organization there would be no Gospel witness in this place." What this argument is really saying is, "The church has failed." It is perhaps true that the work of God is not going forward because some churches are failing at what they should be doing, but it doesn't give us an excuse to give our devotion to a para-church organization instead of or even along side of the local church. *God intended for His work in this dispensation to be carried out through the local church.* There is no other design in the Bible. Acts 1:8 says, "*But ye* [believers] *shall receive power, after that the Holy Ghost is come upon you: and ye* [organized and working together as a local church] *shall be witnesses unto me both in Jerusalem, and in all Judaea, and in Samaria, and unto the uttermost part of the earth.*"

With my life, I am to work at spreading the Gospel, allowing God to do His work through me as a part of the larger work of the local church. My purpose in stating all of this is to encourage everyone to realize that each of us has only one life. He must use it for God's glory working through the one institution He set up to carry out the Great Commission. Time is of the essence, and your local church needs you!

The church that God has given us has everything necessary to carry out the Great Commission. "Well," you say, "not our church. We have a smaller congregation," or "Our church doesn't have much money," or "We don't have as many people." You are shortchanging God. God doesn't need a lot of money. God doesn't need a lot of people to carry out the commission of world evangelism and starting churches. Doing this great work involves looking at who I have and where I am and getting started with what I have. What a privilege and great blessing to be involved in church planting!

A BETTER UNDERSTANDING OF ACTS 1:8

POWER

> *But ye shall receive power, after that the Holy Ghost is come upon you: and ye shall be witnesses unto me both in Jerusalem, and in all Judaea, and in Samaria, and unto the uttermost part of the earth.*—ACTS 1:8

The Greek word for *power* here is *dunamis* from which we get our English word *dynamite*. This is major power that we are talking about. God's work *must* be done through the Holy Spirit, or it will not be done at all. Dynamite connotes explosive power, but the Holy Spirit is also the sustaining power, as is suggested by the word *dynamo*, also a derivative of *dunamis*. Where dynamite is a quick, temporary, explosive discharge of energy, generally destroying the status quo so that something better can be produced, the dynamo is a sustaining source of generated power that keeps the thing to which it is attached working and moving—attributes that we apply to a healthy church.

PEOPLE

Everyone is to be a witness for Jesus Christ. It's interesting that the Greek word for *witness* is *martus* from which we get our English word *martyr*. So when Jesus said *"ye shall be witnesses unto me,"* He actually told us "you shall be martyrs unto Me." The word did not have the exact meaning back then that it does today. It didn't mean that a witness had to die for the Lord, but it meant that he would put his life on the line to be a witness for the Lord. So don't expect witnessing to be some kind of walk in the park. When God told us to "go into all the world," He knew it would take commitment on our part.

PHILOSOPHY

Notice the word *both* in Acts 1:8. The great problem of church planting in our day is that most preachers and churches misinterpret this word to mean *first*. For this very reason many churches begin with the wrong philosophy. The emphasis in the Bible is not on our Jerusalem but on our world. When you go to start a church, all you are thinking about is your one church. You're not thinking about Singapore, Russia, Kenya, or Mexico.

You're not thinking about anything but your little niche. That's only natural. But I say, from day one, make sure that you cover the point of world evangelism. At the same time that you are trying to evangelize your Jerusalem, you should be trying to evangelize your Judaea and Samaria and the uttermost part of the earth.

On the very first Sunday of our church in 1970, we had a budget set up that covered everything including a missions budget of $6.25 per week. My idea was that $25 a month would be sufficient to start participating with other churches in supporting one missionary. (It was enough back then.) Cooperating with other churches of like faith to reach everyone with the Gospel of Jesus Christ is something that every church is responsible to do, including churches that missionaries themselves plant. It is absolutely key that the emphasis be put, not on our Jerusalem, but on the world.

The truth of the matter is that many missionary-evangelists out on the foreign field have the wrong philosophy of missions. You might find that hard to believe. After all, if anyone should be an expert on missions, it should be the missionary-evangelist who is somewhere overseas starting churches. If you were to ask the average missionary how many men he has sent outside his country or how many churches his church has helped to get started in other countries, the answer would probably be few or none. Most have little or no emphasis on evangelizing the world. All they think about is the one country in which they are working, an outlook I can understand. But this kind of tunnel vision needs to change. Even with Paul's love for his own people, he still ministered to the Gentiles.

It's easy to feel that a poor church in a poor third-world country can't do much. But that's not what the Bible says! There's no difference between a church here in the United States and a church overseas. God doesn't differentiate between churches. The wealthy churches don't have one commission and the poor churches another. Every church has the same Great Commission of Matthew 28:19–20, or Mark 16, Luke 24, John 20, or Acts 1:8. Every church has the responsibility—Jerusalem, Judaea, Samaria and the uttermost. The average church on the mission field, just like those here in the States, has no concept of real world evangelism.

PROGRAM

We all understand that when I discuss "Jerusalem," I am talking about reaching your own area. Obviously, that's where your heart is. That's why you are there. Then there is "Judaea," spreading out to our counties and states. "Samaria" is really, in my eyes, reaching the unwanted. When the disciples found Jesus with the woman at the well, they thought it most unusual because the Jews usually went around Samaria when traveling. Samaria is where all the unwanted people lived. They had mixed blood of Jews and Gentiles. The Jews did not like them and would have nothing to do with them, and neither would the Gentiles.

Our door-to door visitation programs are not to be like a buffet where we decide which people we invite and which ones we do not. I have seen people who, as they knock on doors, just don't have the same enthusiasm for some people as they do for others. Looking down on someone who doesn't look or talk just like we do is wrong, sinful, ungodly, wretched, and contrary to Scripture. It's everything that we should not be doing. If God calls you to an area, wherever it is, you are there to reach out to everyone with the Gospel and a heart-felt invitation to your church. This outreach includes all ethnic groups—whites, Hispanics, Asians, or blacks—and it also includes those who are in some way different without regard to ethnicity, such as the deaf, the blind, the physically and mentally challenged, etc. What a great responsibility, but what a wonderful thing.

> **EVERY CHURCH HAS THE SAME GREAT COMMISSION.**

Ethnic diversity is a positive thing, not a negative thing! What a shame to walk into churches and find no ethnic or other types of diversity. I have said many times that one of the strengths of the Fairfax Baptist Temple is its ethnic diversity. It is something you should accept with open arms. There is no way in the world you will have the joy that could be yours unless you have a heart for everyone.

The *uttermost*, spoken of in Acts 1:8, is world evangelism. Has it ever occurred to you that to someone in Europe or Asia the United States is the uttermost? Remember once again that we are to be ministering in each of these areas at the same time.

THE EARLY CHURCH'S CHURCH PLANTING EFFORTS

The early church, as commissioned by God, didn't quite get the responsibility and obligation of the commission that God intended. They resisted at first and did not obey. God then used His own method to spur them.

> *And Saul was consenting unto his death. And at that time there was a great persecution against the church which was at Jerusalem; and they were all scattered abroad throughout the regions of Judaea and Samaria, except the apostles. And devout men carried Stephen to his burial, and made great lamentation over him. As for Saul, he made havock of the church, entering into every house, and haling men and women committed them to prison. Therefore they that were scattered abroad went every where preaching the word.*—ACTS 8:1–4

It is interesting how God got them going. He sent persecution, which motivated the church to get out and do what He had told them to do. He put the fire under them to get them going.

Although there is not a lot of detail about what happened next, we do know that church planting was the result of their going everywhere.

> *Then Philip went down to the city of Samaria, and preached Christ unto them. And the people with one accord gave heed unto those things which Philip spake, hearing and seeing the miracles which he did. For unclean spirits, crying with loud voice, came out of many that were possessed with them: and many taken with palsies, and that were lame, were healed. And there was great joy in that city.*—ACTS 8:5–8

So Philip preached Christ in Samaria, launching the evangelization of the Samaritan people. In verses 12–14 of Acts 8, we see the work progressing and a church established.

> *But when they believed Philip preaching the things concerning the kingdom of God, and the name of Jesus Christ, they were baptized, both men and women. Then Simon himself believed also: and when he was baptized, he continued with Philip and wondered, beholding the miracles and signs which were done. Now when the apostles which were at Jerusalem heard that Samaria had received the word of God, they sent unto them Peter and John.*—ACTS 8:12–14

In verse 25 it says, *"And they, when they had testified and preached the word of the Lord, returned to Jerusalem, and preached the gospel in many villages of the Samaritans."* Here again, Samaria was evangelized through the preaching and ministry of God's Word and through the disciples that went out. God was doing some great works.

Then the church at Antioch started up. *"Now they which were scattered abroad upon the persecution that arose about Stephen travelled as far as Phenice, and Cyprus, and Antioch, preaching the word to none but unto the Jews only"* (Acts 11:19). The church at Antioch became a great sending church.

It wouldn't hurt to underline the phrase *preaching the word* every time you read it in your Bible. When you get ready to build a church (I do understand that Jesus Christ is the one ultimately who builds the church, but perhaps we can help by hauling the bricks!), make sure you build it on the strength of your preaching, which is to say on the strength of the Word of God. If you do it on the strength of your fanfare and excitement and programs, when they run out, so will the people! Build it on the preaching of the Word of God. That's the way they did it in the churches described in the New Testament. New Testament church planters didn't survey the community to find out what they wanted to hear from the pulpit and then build a church to satisfy what the people were seeking. They preached the Word!

*And some of them were men of Cyprus and Cyrene, which, when they were come to Antioch, spake unto the Grecians, preaching the Lord Jesus. And the hand of the Lord was with them: and a great number believed, and turned unto the Lord. Then tidings of these things came unto the ears of the church which was in Jerusalem: and they sent forth Barnabas, that he should go as far as Antioch…And when he had found him, he brought him unto Antioch. And it came to pass, that a whole year they assembled themselves with the church, and taught much people. And the disciples were called Christians first in Antioch.—*ACTS 11:20–22, 26

More church planters were then sent out of the church at Antioch.

Now there were in the church that was at Antioch certain prophets and teachers; as Barnabas, and Simeon that was called Niger; and Lucius of Cyrene and Manaen, which had been brought up with Herod the tetrarch, and Saul. As they ministered to the Lord

and fasted, the Holy Ghost said, Separate me Barnabas
and Saul for the work whereunto I have called them.
And when they had fasted and prayed, and laid their
hands on them, they sent them away. So they, being
sent forth by the Holy Ghost, departed unto Seleucia;
and from thence they sailed to Cyprus. And when they
were at Salamis, they preached the word of God in the
synagogues of the Jews: and they had also John to their
minister.—ACTS 13:1–5

Then Paul and Barnabas, who were sent out, continued to start churches and to minister to the churches in Lystra, Iconium and Derbe. Paul and Silas started the church at Philippi in Acts 16. The church at Thessalonica was started in Acts 17.

CONCLUDING THOUGHT

The heart of the Great Commission is church planting. This must be the heart of every pastor and every church, for every church has been given the same responsibility—to evangelize the world by starting churches. It is God's only plan; therefore, we must never replace church planting with anything else. Churches must take care to set aside the time, money, and manpower to obey God at any cost, and we need to continue doing so for the Lord Jesus Christ.

> CHURCH
> PLANTING IS
> NOT OPTIONAL.

Church planting is not optional. To be a church planter is a high and holy calling of God. Never take this calling for granted or treat it lightly. If you are called of God to start churches, praise the Lord that you can be involved in this process. What a blessing! It is very humbling to think that God could use any one of us to start a church for which His holy Son died. Christ's sacrifice makes what we do extremely important in the mind of God. *"Therefore, my beloved brethren, be ye stedfast, unmovable, always abounding in the work of the Lord, forasmuch as ye know that your labour is not in vain in the Lord"* (1 Corinthians 15:58).

THE RESPONSIBILITY
TO REPRODUCE

We have seen that the heart of the Great Commission is church planting. This is the God-ordained way to evangelize the world, to carry forth His life-saving message to mankind. It is the only method with the authority of the Word of God behind it. The Bible says the *"...gates of hell shall not prevail against it"* (Matthew 16:18). Nothing should ever replace church planting. It is here to stay.

Carrying out the Great Commission and starting churches is not the responsibility of individuals, denominations, mission boards, educational institutions, or para-church organizations. It is the job of the church. So what are the responsibilities of the church in carrying out the Great Commission? Exactly what does God expect a church to do in order to begin this great work? To follow the biblical pattern, the church must first pray.

Prayer should be made for the needs of the entire world. Keep in mind that *"God so loved the world"* (John 3:16). He does not just love America. *"God is no respecter of persons"* (Acts 10:34).

PRAYER

We cannot begin to think about being fruitful in our efforts to evangelize the world if we leave God out of our efforts. It is God who will supply. If you are an established pastor, and no one has been called out of your ministry to be a church planter, it may be that you have not pleaded with God to make it happen. *"Ye have not because ye ask not"* (James 4:2). If you think that your church does not have the financial or other resources necessary, perhaps you have not knocked hard enough and long enough on Heaven's door. *"Hitherto have ye asked nothing in my name: ask, and ye shall receive, that your joy may be full"* (John 16:24). A pastor in the States or a missionary-evangelist overseas should not be content to work with someone else's preachers-in-training but should pray that God would give him some of his own. The typical church, in order to develop a missions program, waits for missionaries to come through and then takes them on for support. Supporting missionaries is good. But, if you are the pastor of a church, or even a member, I challenge you to pray that God will raise up a man from your *own* church whom you can send out. Prayer should be made for more laborers. Our Lord said, *"…The harvest truly is plenteous, but the labourers are few; Pray ye therefore the Lord of the harvest, that he will send forth labourers into his harvest"* (Matthew 9:37–38). Two quick observations can be made. The first is that the harvest truly is plenteous. The second is that the laborers are few.

There is no problem with the harvest field. It is plenteous. The problem is with the laborers. God tells the church to pray specifically that He, God, would send laborers. So keep praying for laborers to go and for God to work in the lives of people who want to get involved in God's work. Pastor, you must challenge each one in your congregation to pray specifically that *he* will be that next laborer whom God sends. Be honest with yourself before God. When was the last time you seriously prayed for God to raise up more laborers and church planters out of your congregation? I don't do it as often as I ought to either. Do you want more laborers? Pray. Do you want more helpers?

> PRAY THAT GOD WILL RAISE UP A MAN FROM YOUR OWN CHURCH WHOM YOU CAN SEND OUT.

Pray! Do you want to be a sending church? Pray! If you are a church planter, begin praying now, even before you get your church started, that God will use the church you will soon pastor to be a sending church. Regardless of what you do in the church, please start praying, and pray daily, for God to raise up more church planters and laborers for His harvest field. Lack of prayer results in a lack of laborers.

I hear regularly about closed countries. We call a country closed because the government in that place will not welcome a missionary-evangelist to come and start churches. Typically, what I have seen among some Christians is the attitude that they can't go to a particular place because it is closed. But my question is who closed it? It wasn't God, because we know from the Bible that God loves *"...the world"* (John 3:16), and we know He is *"...not willing that any should perish..."* (2 Peter 3:9). The devil may be trying to close countries, but God isn't. Perhaps these countries have, not a "closed" door, but a "stuck" door that needs some men of faith to walk on through! The obstacle may appear difficult, but God asks, *"Behold, I am the LORD, the God of all flesh: is there any thing too hard for me?"* (Jeremiah 32:27).

One's perception of a country as closed in no way relieves the church of the responsibility to go into that country. The pastor whose heart has been stirred by God with concern for the people of a closed place simply has to figure out a way to get the Gospel in. Here again, prayer is the answer. There is no better way to get workers into closed countries than praying for God to lead you and your church to find emigrants from those countries who could potentially be trained and sent back to start a church in their native land. That is one of the thrilling things about being in the Washington, D.C. area where we have a diverse multicultural population. It is possible to get someone from China to go back to China, or someone from the Middle East to go back to his home country.

Unfortunately, I don't think a whole lot is being done to figure out ways to get into these countries. One does not have to go in with the declaration of being a church planter to be biblical. It could be that he goes in as a farmer, businessman, or schoolteacher, but he should be there as a church planter first and as a businessman or schoolteacher second. I've heard of groups that try to get people into a country to teach English.

That has always been the way to get into China. If he goes, he mustn't go just to teach English, unless, of course, he has not been gifted as a pastor or an evangelist, in which case, he should not expect his work to be supported by churches as a missions effort. No church has enough missions money to support works that are not involved in church planting. He should go as a church planter who is using teaching school as a means to a greater end.

If you have a burden for the Chinese and you just have to go, then go. Work in the school to get contacts and leads, and then, eventually, do what you can to get a church started, even if it means being expelled some day.

One of my staff ministers told me of a young man who went into an Arabic-speaking country as an electrician with the purpose of training nationals in his trade, his primary purpose, of course, being evangelism. He was there a number of years before being forced to leave. He moved to another country where he could use his language skills and started evangelizing there.

We cannot quit thinking and praying about getting into closed countries and starting churches just because the god of this world has set up barriers through human government. God is not limited except by our lack of prayer.

PROMOTION

We must begin to think in terms of providing more laborers. Our churches must get everyone thinking about the possibility of being part of starting a church—sending or being sent. The average man in your congregation may be listening to you and thinking, "I just don't know if I have a burden from God to start a church." I say that every man ought to figure out exactly why, from the Bible, he is *not* going to go start a church. The Bible says to every Christian, *"Go ye therefore and teach all nations"* (Matthew 28:19); *"Go ye into all the world and preach the Gospel to every creature"* (Mark 16:15); *"Ye shall be witness unto me"* (Acts 1:8). So, challenge your members with a series of rhetorical questions such as, "If you are not already an active soulwinner, why aren't you? If you are, why not pray to God that He would privilege you to be a church planter?"

To be honest with you, there are answers in the Bible as to why some should *not* go and start a church. For instance, someone may consider going, but after examining his gifts and calling, he may realize that he is not called or equipped to go. If God has not gifted or called him to do so, it is foolish for him to try. Although he may care, God has not burdened or called him.

I believe that there are not many men thinking about going. In the average church today, the people, including parents and children, look at the pastor and think, "He has his job, and we have ours." Is this type of thinking being challenged? Are they being challenged to think that maybe they could be the next family to go? As the pastor, I would encourage every biblically qualified man to think about the possibility of starting a church either here in America or on a foreign field. I would encourage parents to realize that their children are God's to lead and direct, and to teach their children to esteem the work of the ministry as the highest vocation they could undertake. How sad that some parents do their best to direct their children into sports or computer vocations without even considering the ministry.

One of the men on my staff has a single daughter who is working with church planters in Uganda. He told me that he called the mission board affiliated with the missionary-evangelist who, in addition to planting churches, was managing the orphanage in which she would be working. He called to inquire how he might encourage his daughter along the way. His inquiry was met with a moment of silence. The country director then apologized for the delayed response, confessing that he had anticipated the call to be from yet one more father asking for help to discourage his daughter from the mission field. That is a sad commentary. Five years later, this young woman testifies of the extreme joy that comes

> CHURCHES MUST GET EVERYONE THINKING ABOUT THE POSSIBILITY OF BEING PART OF STARTING A CHURCH.

from knowing she is exactly where God would have her, doing exactly what He would have her do. You could never tell me there is anything that could bring more satisfaction to a father's heart.

Pastor, to fully accomplish your equipping task as set out in Ephesians 4, preach on the need of the world from the pulpit regularly. I encourage all men and boys to consider the call. We need to help them to know what the call is. It is mainly an overwhelming desire for the work of the ministry ("...*If a man desire the office of a bishop, he desireth a good work*" —1 Timothy 3:1). It is a burden that is hard to release. It is a "*woe is unto me, if I preach not*" situation (1 Corinthians 9:16). I encourage our young ladies to be willing to be missionaries' or pastors' wives and in seeking a husband to look for a young man with the ministry as a first priority in his life's goals.

Have an emphasis on church planting in your youth group. Highlight the men and boys who are called. My favorite ensemble in our church is the men and boys group who have been called into the ministry. (It's not their singing that touches my heart; it's the fact that they are surrendered to the Lord!)

Recruit others to go with you when you start churches. Take youth and adult groups overseas to visit the mission fields when you go. Doing so can get them stirred up for the ministry and passionate for church planting themselves.

It was eight years after we started the Fairfax Baptist Temple that my wife and I took our first overseas missions trip. We went for nineteen days to Japan, Korea, Hong Kong, and the Philippines. While we were there, we visited missionary-evangelists who were all strong church planters. It was very exciting to see and meet these men and to hear the testimonies of how they started various churches. God used this trip to move my heart. *"Mine eye affecteth my heart..."* (Lamentations 3:51). Once you see and taste the mission field for yourself, it will revolutionize your heart and your thinking. I saw little Filipino children who live in cardboard huts with their parents and who took baths in the street after a heavy rainfall. We saw tens of thousands of people in Hong Kong with no direction in their lives, the millions in the little country of Japan with few to show them the right way.

That trip was a turning point for me; it was then that I began to understand the spiritual need in the world. I came back and decided that we were going to change our missions philosophy completely. At that time, our missions giving was provided through our budget. Then we switched over to *faith promise*, or what we now call *grace giving* (discussed in chapter 9). As a result of the change in our financial procedures, we have seen millions more given for world evangelism.

Man of God, walk closely with the Lord, begging him for a genuine burden for world evangelism. This is the greatest promotional method I know of for stirring up a church. If you get a burden in your heart, you will not be able to hide it from others.

TRAINING

The tremendous shortage of servants willing to go and plant churches is, in my mind, largely due to very little challenge from the pulpit to yield one's life for service to the King. Another reason is the wrong philosophy in many of our church schools. Many churches are on defense against public schools instead of being on offense, training servants for the work of the Lord. So many church schools are started as a reaction to government schools. But opposing public education should not be the primary reason a church starts a school. The primary reason should be a desire to come alongside parents as they train their children to be servants of God.

Don't misunderstand. I'm against the typical public school system mainly because the curriculum is decidedly anti-God. That is, there is no public school that teaches a God-centered course of study, lifting up Christ's holy name in science, math, literature, and every other course it offers. Public schools will not offer courses that teach personal evangelism or world evangelism or the Bible as God's inspired Word. The warning of Scripture can't be any plainer when it teaches, *"Beware lest any man spoil you through philosophy and vain deceit, after the tradition of men, after the rudiments of the world, and not after Christ"* (Colossians 2:8). The phrase *"not after Christ"* is a perfect definition of secular humanism, the kind of training our young people need to avoid. (I do, however, understand exceptions, and I trust parents' decisions in putting some students with special needs, learning disabilities, autism, etc., in public school where they can get one-on-one attention.)

As I said earlier, our church school exists because we want to train young people to be servants of God. We want to get them on the offense. I want all of our young people to be thinking about serving the Lord. I agree with Moses who said, *"...would God that all the Lord's people were prophets, and that the Lord would put his spirit upon them!"* (Numbers 11:29). By the way, Moses said this in a training session with his men.

Sadly, some Christian schools (the difference between a church school and a Christian school is whether the pastor of the church is the real head of the school or whether a board or other governing entity is running the school) are not much different from the public schools in the emphasis they place on high-tech careers, because "that's where the money is!" But what does that have to do with fulfilling life's purpose? Also, in Christian or church schools today there is often an unbalanced emphasis on sports. I like a sports program, but I don't like it to usurp the ministry program. The students who stand out in the school ought to be the ones who are dedicated to ministry, not the high-scoring basketball or soccer players. The highlight of the year should be some event that is decidedly spiritual as opposed to athletic.

If we want to produce young men and ladies fit for the ministry, then we may have to change the course of our church schools and youth groups. Our teen ministry at church should constantly be pointing young people toward developing their gifts for service to our Lord. The church school and youth ministry should be pro-active in training young people to be witnesses for the Lord. Pastor, teach your young people to develop their character after the principles of God's Word and the godly examples of Scriptures, and make the ministry something to be desired, not dreaded!

SEPARATION

Another reason for the shortage of laborers is the adverse influence of secular activities, especially when these take a place of priority. One of the biggest intrusions between parents and children is television. In so many homes today the television is on hours upon hours at a time. This preoccupation with television kills the Holy Spirit's work in young people's lives, as well as in their parents' lives. It stifles conversation, and it dulls the mind. The chances of encountering something that is an insult to their faith, purity, or desire for righteousness are infinitely greater than the chances of having those things affirmed and supported because the values reinforced in the great majority of programming are decidedly anti-Christian.

The clear admonition of Scriptures is *"Love not the world, neither the things that are in the world. If any man love the world the love of the Father is not in him"* (1 John 2:15). Rather than asking the familiar question, "What's wrong with it?" we should be teaching the principle of separation from a positive perspective. Instruct your people to evaluate their amusements and activities by asking, "What's right with it?" A love affair with this world will put one on a slippery slope toward becoming what Paul called a "castaway," one disapproved by God.

PREACHER'S INTERNSHIP PROGRAM

Let me direct these next thoughts primarily to you who are already serving our Lord as pastor of a church. I highly recommend that you, as pastors and missionaries, consider the possibility of providing an internship program for every man whom God calls into the ministry through your church. As their pastor, your influence, mentoring, and training in the lives of your ministry bound men is the most significant. Provide this also for men going into the ministry who marry young ladies from your church. The internship should be at least one year in length with the possibility of extending it to two or three years, depending on the variables of each situation.

One of the greatest privileges I know is to have God call someone from your church into the ministry. Church planting, by the way, is not the only ministry to which men may be called. I believe most of those whom we title "assistant pastors" are also what the Bible refers to as elders or bishops. There may be some differences in our ministry functions, but it is the same God who does the calling.

The internship program can be paid for from the missions program since it is not for the benefit of your church, although your church will be blessed by this program. Our purpose for having the internship program is for the benefit of the interns, not our own. That's why we don't use them as full-time janitors or schoolteachers. We usually have them teach a Bible class in our school, but we don't require them to teach three hours a day, five days a week and call that an internship. That's a schoolteacher's job. We don't use them for our benefit. Our purpose is to teach them as many phases of the ministry as possible.

At Fairfax Baptist Temple, the Intern Program tasks are designed to give the intern relevant information and practical work experience as a pastor or missionary-evangelist starting a new church. Experience is gained primarily through fulfilling a rigorous requirement for personal visitation, meeting regularly with the ministerial

A LOVE AFFAIR WITH THIS WORLD WILL PUT ONE ON A SLIPPERY SLOPE.

staff to discuss the staff member's areas of ministry oversight, preparing sermons and other teaching materials, reading a list of books that has proven useful to ministerial staff members, and developing a ministry plan (the intern's specific plan for starting his church). The intern will find that he has to work an irregular schedule to accomplish all of these activities. This lesson is important for the church planter in training.

One of the very important aspects of the training is meticulous inquiry into the intern's Bible knowledge and beliefs. For at least an hour each day the intern meets with one of the ministerial staff who asks him questions designed to force the intern to think beyond the superficial clichés that all too often are given without much explanation. The ministerial staff person will take contrary positions, requiring the intern to defend the faith once delivered. For all the men, but especially for the interns going to places where Christianity is not the dominant religion, this preparation is designed to instill confidence. As much as I can, I want the interns to have been confronted with the most difficult questions he will ever be asked by any skeptic or practitioner of the world's false religions. (After these sessions, the ordination council can be a truly enjoyable experience!)

PASTOR OR MISSIONARY-EVANGELIST?

Having the right man to send out, obviously, is the key to the whole endeavor of churches starting churches. While most men sent out directly from your church will have the privilege of going through your internship program, others may be ready to go to the mission field directly from college or may be otherwise ready to start a church without the internship program. They should still follow the ministry plan of preparation for the endeavor ahead.

Before discussing the church's role in preparing the candidates to be sent out, I want to examine the distinction between the two calls of church planters. Part of preparing these men is helping them distinguish their gifts and the specific call of God on their lives so that they accomplish the life's work God has designed them to do.

There was a man who came to preach at our church years ago who was going to the mission field. For some reason we didn't get him fully screened prior to his coming, so I invited him into my office. While he was telling me about going to Canada I asked, "What do you plan to do when you get on the field?"

He said, "Plant churches."

I concluded that this guy was right on target. "Wonderful!" I said, "How are you going to do it?"

He said, "Well, I'm going to go start a church. Eventually, I want to see some men from that church called to preach. Then I'm going to set up a Bible institute to train them. Upon graduation, I will help them start their own churches. I will continue pastoring, seeing men called, trained, and then send them out as well."

I said, "I praise the Lord that you are going to Canada to start churches. I've got one question for you though. When I came to Fairfax, my family and I started a church by faith. Eventually, I had some men called into the ministry. We started our own Bible institute, trained them, and helped them start churches as I continued to pastor the Fairfax Baptist Temple. My question is, why do they call me a pastor and you a missionary? If we are doing exactly the same thing, what is the distinguishing factor that makes you a missionary and me a pastor? Is it going across the border or a body of water that makes you a missionary?"

I then asked him what his spiritual gift was. Although he had taught in a Bible college for a while, he responded "I don't know. I've never thought about it." How unfortunate. Knowing his spiritual gift determines a man's goal for his church.

Please understand, we are very sympathetic toward those men who go to countries where it is very difficult to win someone to the Lord, let alone start a church. We are extremely patient toward any man who may take a long time to finally see a church built and turned over to a national, if he is in a difficult country. However, when he starts running over a hundred or even hundreds, it is our understanding that he should turn that work over to a well-prepared national and be moving on as soon as possible. We don't support pastors on a permanent basis just because they are going across the border. A missionary must have the mindset of working himself out of a job, or he is not a true missionary-evangelist seeking to build an indigenous (self-governing, self-supporting, and self-propagating) church, in the way I understand it.

> A MISSIONARY MUST HAVE THE MINDSET OF WORKING HIMSELF OUT OF A JOB.

On my first trip to a mission field overseas, I noticed that the missionaries there were serving in one of two distinct ways. The men in one of those two groups were serving the church in the role of pastor, but they were not holding the office of pastor. These men were continually working themselves out of a job. The men in the other group were those who were starting a church, staying with it, and letting it grow big. These men occupied the office of pastor with no intent of turning it over to a national until they were ready to return to the United States. The men in both groups thought they were doing it right and the men in the other group were doing it wrong. That's what got me thinking, "Well, which *is* the right way?"

I think that, as a U.S.-based pastor or a missionary-evangelist in some other country, you can go start a church, pray for and see God give you men He has called to preach, train them in your church, and send them out. However, if your calling is that of missionary-evangelist, I don't think you should stay around as pastor of that church for very long. There is a difference in the heart of a man who, as a missionary-evangelist, starts a church, sees people saved, invests himself in their lives, and then turns it all over to a national and leaves to start the process again and yet again from a pastor who cannot think about leaving the work he started. But what sometimes happens, perhaps, is that the missionary-evangelist becomes comfortable and thinks, "Hey, I like this getting bigger business. My family is comfortable and loved here. Perhaps I should just stay." I understand the allure, but staying to pastor is not the gift or call of the missionary-evangelist.

When Paul was encouraging Timothy as a young pastor, he wrote to him *"But watch thou in all things, endure afflictions, **do the work of an evangelist,** make full proof of thy ministry"* (2 Timothy 4:5, emphasis mine). It is my understanding that a pastor should stay involved in the church planting process like the evangelist does. A pastor is to work to evangelize his Jerusalem, the area extending from his church, and then reach out beyond his church, seeking to start other churches. The missionary-evangelist, on the other hand, goes to unfurrowed ground and plants a church, intending from the beginning to move on. This is what Paul did when he went into the city to get his leadership for each church.

As long as the American is pastoring the church on foreign soil, he does not have an indigenous church, which should be the goal of every church planter and sending church. I simply want to put us in mind that an indigenous church is self-supporting, self-governing, and self-propagating. Although the missionary-evangelist and pastor do the same things in the beginning, if one is overseas somewhere, the church will not be indigenous as long as he is leading the church and receiving support from American churches. Any church receiving money from the United States is not indigenous, which is why we do not interfere with the process of churches learning to look to God for their supply instead of to American churches.

Every man, regardless of his specific calling, needs a plan in order to meet success. The following are things the sending pastor and church will need to develop and understand with the church planter:

HIS CALL OF GOD AND HIS GIFTS

Paul, while writing his son in the faith, said, *"And I thank Christ Jesus our Lord, who hath enabled me, for that he counted me faithful, putting me into the ministry"* (1 Timothy 1:12). Paul had proven himself with faithful service when the Lord, who knew his heart as He does ours, put him in the ministry. In dealing with a candidate for the ministry, the pastor must ascertain his calling from God. Regardless of the man's spiritual ambitions, talents, or abilities, he must acknowledge the call of God as something different. The call must emanate from God's heart, not man's.

As the sending pastor, you will want to help the candidate for ministry service understand his spiritual gift(s). (You will want his wife to know her gift[s] as well.) There are tests available that reveal areas of particular interest. If the candidate does not score very high in the categories of teaching and hospitality, according to 1 Timothy 3, he may not be suited for the office of bishop. In the simple test I have used for years, there are questions that tend to show giftedness for the office of pastor or as an evangelist. The difference is found largely in the response to those questions related to a heart's desire for people of an ethnic group that is not the candidate's own, an inclination to leave his home country, and a heart and mind disposed to the idea of foreign missions.

HIS PASSION

This heart element is of utmost importance. When considering a man to go and start a church, whether in the United States or overseas, a pastor needs to make sure the man is "chompin' at the bit"! An excitement or spirit of anticipation should be clearly apparent. Paul put it this way, *"For though I preach the gospel, I have nothing to glory of: for necessity is laid upon me; yea, woe is unto me, if I preach not the gospel!"* (1 Corinthians 9:16). This "necessity" or conviction must be part of the very fabric of the man being considered for commissioning from the church.

HIS OVERALL PERSONALITY AND DEMEANOR

If there is something that could be a potential hindrance, work on it together. Being a Bible college graduate or, more importantly, being called of God does not necessarily mean that one's character and personality has been perfected! The sending pastor and church need to make sure that the rough edges have been smoothed as much as possible. The man you send out as God's representative and yours must know how to carry himself with grace and strength. For example, if he will be ministering in an area where the residents are educated people, he needs to be especially careful that his grammar and communication skills are good. As the sending pastor, you need to try to discern if the candidate going to a different culture is likely to adapt easily. Do not ignore the candidate's wife and family in this evaluation.

MANNERS—HIS RELATIONSHIP AND ETHICS WITH OTHER PASTORS

Make sure that the man who will be sent out from your church is very ethical and forthright in all that he does. Especially in the case of a man who is going to an area where churches are already established, help him to meet and explain his intentions to the pastors of like-minded churches in the area. Instruct him to inform local pastors when someone from their churches visits his church. Experienced pastors know that people are going to go to church where they want to go for a variety of different (sometimes even spiritual) reasons. As much as we pastors would like to, we will not be able to keep everyone that visits or joins the church. That's just the way it is. You can model ethics for the man you are sending out by again being careful when someone visits your church to let the visitor's pastor know that one of his members has visited. It has been my practice not to conduct a follow-up visit with those people unless their present pastor is aware that some of his own members are looking at other churches. I don't let people come from sister churches and run down their former pastor because I know if they'll do that to him, they'll do the same to me. Ethics are important.

HIS ABILITY TO WORK WITH PEOPLE

The ministry is a people vocation. Since "people" are the ones he will be working with, the man you are sending must know, as much as possible, how to manage, love, help, guide, and encourage others. A great study for anyone would be to examine the Bible references on "one anothering," which establish a baseline for ministry. From this study, the man will learn that if he wants to be a leader, he must show himself worthy of being followed. Above all else, the job of the pastor or missionary-evangelist is to love the people whom God has given him.

The best way for him to learn and develop the ability to work with people is to place the candidate in situations that demand this adeptness from him. There are many ways to let the candidate gain some practical firsthand experience. Arrange for him to make hospital visits, which kindle compassion in him. Require the candidate to develop programs that he then has to carry out with the elderly or the disadvantaged. Involve him in a meaningful way in the process of assimilating new members. Have him work as a mentor to the children of single parents. Engage him in one-on-one discipleship. In short, make sure that the candidate is involved in meeting the variety of needs that the people of your congregation have.

HIS ABILITY TO RESOLVE PROBLEMS

This is absolutely essential in what we are doing. Here is an absolute "must" for anyone aspiring to the office of pastor. Among other things, I have always believed that a pastor or missionary-evangelist must be a problem solver, resolving not only his own but others' as well. When church problems occur, and they will, or when someone brings in an interpersonal problem, such as a marriage or work problem, the pastor will be expected to resolve it. In these situations, the man of God must fully understand the problem, search the Scriptures for an answer, and apply it to the problem at hand. A key passage for a pastor to keep in mind is 2 Peter 1:3, telling us that we depend upon God who *"according as his divine power hath given unto us all things that pertain unto life and godliness, through the knowledge of him that hath called us to glory and virtue."*

It is hard to give the candidate experience in counseling. Most of the time, when a person or a couple comes to a church for counsel they are not open to having another person sitting in to listen. Generally, they want to speak only to the pastor. There are also legitimate legal concerns to consider if the counselee wishes to preserve the privileged nature of the communication.

While it is not as good as the real thing, perhaps doing some role playing exercises will give you the opportunity to see how the candidate thinks and responds. You may be able to enlist some members of the church to be "actors" so that there is a real dynamic to the role playing.

HIS MANAGEMENT PHILOSOPHY

This is an inquiry into his overall work habits and time management. As the sending pastor, you want to answer the following questions. Is he capable of managing his own time? Is he capable of getting out on the field and dealing with God's work? Does his wife have to get him out of bed every morning, or is he a self-starter?

Remind the candidate wanting to start a church that at the outset of his ministry, he will have a small church, and he will be the only salaried staff member. He and his wife, for the most part, will be the ones doing the work of the ministry. Require him to answer a few questions. To whom will he be accountable? How disciplined is he?

When I started the Fairfax Baptist Temple no one was looking over my shoulder or checking up on me, though there was One to whom I would give an account for the work I did. For the new pastor and perhaps especially for the man going overseas, it is imperative that he has good work habits.

For most men starting a church, their office is going to be in their bedroom or kitchen—nothing fancy. The man of God must discipline himself to be in that "office" at a certain time every day and learn how to avoid interruptions. A husband and wife must, together, think through what their guidelines will be as they try to be understanding of one another's needs. I've always thought that the family ought to work as quickly as possible to remove the "church office" from their home. It could be that once they get started, they will find a businessman in the church who has extra office space somewhere.

HIS THOUGHTS CONCERNING MUSIC
IN THE CHURCH

What I have in mind as I write this is music that is a part of the worship service. As I drive past churches in communities all across the United States, I readily notice that many churches of all denominational stripes advertise "contemporary" services or "traditional" services or both. I think that it is fair to say that the major difference between the two services is the music. (The relative casualness of attire may also be a significant difference.) I assume that when a pastor decides to offer his congregation a choice, he has determined that, with either style, the congregation is drawn closer to God in holiness and the people are instructed from the Word of God concerning how to live righteous separated lives. I think that because music in the church service serves the very important function of preparing hearts to receive the preached Word, it must be scrutinized by the standards just mentioned.

In working with the men eventually sent out from Fairfax Baptist Temple, I want to be sure that the man has a music philosophy grounded in the Word. Sending pastors, because the commissioned man is sent out to plant a church that resembles yours in both faith and practice, you will want to make sure that the young pastor's philosophy is not contrary to yours, even if it is not exactly the same. If the man will conduct his services in a way that prevents you from wholeheartedly recommending anyone to attend those services, then this is a difference that should prevent you from sponsoring that man as a church planter.

The man going to another country, another culture, has to be careful not to judge what he hears by his standards, or by what his western ear is accustomed to hearing. The standard has to be holiness. The standard has to be whether the music is helping prepare the hearts of the people to receive instruction from the Word of God or whether it is feeding the flesh. It is not defensible to allow fleshly music into the church simply because the sound is familiar to the ears of the particular culture. Wherever we are, we must define music biblically with holiness as the standard.

HIS MISSIONS PHILOSOPHY

Pastor, when your church considers sending out a man to start another church, make sure he has God's global vision for the world. Make sure he has a vision not just for his town, his state, his country, but for the world. I'm thrilled when I meet missionary-evangelists who are excited to go to Kenya, Columbia, or Japan or to whatever country God may be leading them. But we need to keep in mind that wherever they go, they still need to have a global vision for world evangelism.

What happens so often is that men go out to start churches, maybe in a rural area or poor country, and pick up the attitude that they just can't do that much or that God's expectations of them are far less than of those who pastor in the States.

One time I was preaching in a missions conference and the pastor asked me ahead of time about our church missions program. Because he asked me, I told him about it. Later, when he introduced me, he told the congregation, "They give this much money and support this many missionaries. We could never do that," he said, "but certainly, we could do more than we are doing," After I preached, I got in his car with him to go to his house for dessert. The first thing I said was, "Preacher, do you remember what you told your people when you introduced me? Do you know what you taught your people in that one split moment? You taught them that God is a respecter of persons—that God will do in Fairfax something He *won't* do in your town." That's dead wrong and bad theology. If He wants to, God will do more in a remote part of the Amazon jungle than He will in Fairfax, Virginia. God can do anything. Don't put God in a box. If you try it, you will be the one who is disappointed. Help the young pastors you send out to develop veracious attitudes about God and His power.

CHURCH PLANTING METHODOLOGY

It is important for you as the sending pastor to ensure that you and the man you are sending out are in general agreement on his plans for planting a church and pastoring. There is no one way of planting a church, but certainly there should be agreement on *how* it will be done so that there can be synergy among those involved. It is good to sit down ahead of time (at least three to six months out) and discuss exactly what and how things are to be done. Some of the things I always discuss with the fellows we send are these:

THE IMPORTANCE OF DOOR-TO-DOOR VISITATION

What is the specific plan for canvassing the area surrounding the initial meeting place and the area where the man hopes to become permanently established? How does the new pastor intend to involve members of the sending church?

THE LABOR FORCE

Within the new community, is there already a nucleus with which to start? Some of the men sent out of Fairfax Baptist Temple have gone to their childhood home community while others have gone where there is a cluster of relatives. Still others have gone to a place with which they have had no prior connection. Each of these scenarios has a unique set of opportunities and challenges. If there is a nucleus of people awaiting the new work, then there is already a labor force on hand to do some of the initial preparatory work.

PRINTED LITERATURE

What is the new pastor planning for printed literature? Immediately there is a question of quantity and content. Thought needs to be given to the kind of literature that is produced (postcards, flyers, brochures, booklets, tracts).

FINANCES

There will need to be an open discussion regarding finances as well. Chapter 6 covers this in detail.

MONEY

A word to the candidate regarding finances: Your personal finances need to be in order. That means NO DEBT. I won't even pray about sending a man into the ministry if he is carrying a big financial debt. It seems a little skewed for a man to represent himself as a servant of God when that man is demonstrating that he hasn't sufficient patience or trust in God to live within his financial means. If you have large credit card debt, a school bill, a car to pay off, or whatever else, then how are you going to preach and teach God's counsel on financial management with any credibility? My attitude is that you need to work until you get the debt paid off. God's people didn't create the debt load; you did.

As a sending pastor, I think that making sure there is no debt and that the candidate has a good understanding and philosophy about money is one of the most important things I can do.

The sending pastor should be the final one who determines if the church planter is ready to go and then recommends him to the congregation. Finishing an intern program is no guarantee that the church is going to send the intern out. But what you want to do is work with him to make him ready.

REPRODUCING COMES WITH A PRICE

Whatever God orders, He pays for. Since church planting is not an option for a New Testament church, be assured that God will supply the resources. The church at Philippi was clearly a church that was concerned about starting other churches. In 2 Corinthians 8:1, the Apostle Paul used the testimony of the church at Philippi as an example: *"Moreover, brethren, we do you to wit of the grace of God bestowed on the churches of Macedonia."* He wanted to tell the Corinthians about God's grace and goodness in the church at Philippi and in the other churches of Macedonia as well. Here was a church that had a wonderful testimony. To me, Philippians is one of the most exciting books in the Bible to preach and teach. It is a happy book! I believe the text teaches that it is because of their concern for church planting that God gave them the promise (which is ours as well, if we are involved in world evangelism): *"But my God shall supply all your need according to His riches in glory by Christ Jesus"* (Philippians 4:19).

The context of this verse is that Philippi, in their excitement about what God was doing, generously supported Paul and his church planting ministry. Under the inspiration of God, the Apostle Paul says here that their love for the Lord and their desire to advance the work of God was demonstrated as they gave money to help him start other churches. Because of their generosity, God would make sure all of *their* needs were supplied. This promise was given to a giving church—a church so concerned about world evangelism that they gave to start other churches.

Planting churches in the United States is an expensive proposition. It costs quite a bit of money. While church planting in the States is of primary importance, sending out a new church planter should not drain all of the church's resources for world evangelism. Every church will have to think through how much they can afford to invest in a couple as they go out to start a new church.

Churches have different ideas and opinions on this matter, but I think all will agree that it's a thrilling opportunity for a church to be involved in seeing a new work begun. Some sending churches are able to fully support the man that is sent for at least a year. Some of our churches are able to take on a sizeable portion of a church planter's salary and help the couple get to the field a whole lot faster. Other churches are able to help a little but expect the new pastor to work part-time until the church is able to care for his salary.

Like-minded churches can participate in the support of the U.S. church planter, just as they do for the missionary-evangelist going overseas. The difference is that the duration of support for the stateside church planter will be linked to the progress of the church or fixed for a period of time, after which the U.S. church planter will have to seek secular employment if the church is not of sufficient size to support him. We have frequently helped support a man from another area church for his first year or two.

Generally, missionary-evangelists in foreign countries have no opportunity to work in the local economy. The support commitment that is made to a missionary-evangelist is a long-term (until the rapture!) commitment. At one point in the history of Fairfax Baptist Temple, I cut staff pay so that we would be able to continue our support commitment to the men depending upon us.

The new church planter will need to make himself available for six months to go to churches to raise support. If he is working as an intern, maybe he could work it out to go out and raise support while employed there. More than likely, any church that can afford an internship program is also a church where the pastor knows quite a few other pastors in the area. If he attends some preacher fellowships, he could easily meet twenty-five or thirty pastors and let them know of the new church starting. Pastors, encourage your man to continue contacting pastors until he has every service time filled with a speaking opportunity.

The financial preparations for going to a destination overseas will likely require more time and effort. While for some deputation is a "necessary evil," it could instead be a great and wonderful opportunity to go to many different churches to present

WHATEVER GOD ORDERS, HE PAYS FOR.

a challenge for one's specific field of service! As a sending pastor, challenge those going on deputation to apply themselves to stay with it until the task is finished. Set up an agreeable timeframe or expectation with the man on deputation concerning when he should be finished with raising support. Do not allow the time to drag on.

Please forgive me if this sounds like I have an ax to grind, because I do! It seems to me that the way we do furlough today needs a major overhaul. Now, I know there are some exceptions out there; we need, however, to rethink the "four years on the field and one year off the field" concept. It is taught today that this formula is entitled to the missionary! Not so. It is a much outdated non-necessity that needs to be tossed out with cassette tapes. Unfortunately, I cannot find out how this concept started or who started it, but I would think that it originated because of disease and health issues for which the missionary needed some R and R. Back in the mid 1900s there was also the problem of transportation. It took up to 30 days to travel by boat to some of the distant countries, but now we can travel to anywhere in the world in about a day's time.

With the existing formula of four years on and one off, we have about one-third of the total missionary population—counting the couples on deputation—at home in the States at any given time! I am simply asking, how much more could be done for the cause of Christ if only about 10 percent were home at any given time? I think most pastors would love to hear from a missionary who said he wanted to wait another five or ten years before coming back for a six-month furlough. With the ease of communications today and the increase of technology, I would think that most pastors and churches would gladly accept a DVD, phone call, or other means of communication in order for a missionary-evangelist to be able to extend his stay on the field. I say, "Praise the Lord!" But we rarely ever get letters like that.

PEOPLE

There may be church members who get burdened to move with the new pastor to be part of his church. My son, Pastor Troy, and I both have encouraged families to go with one of our new church planting pastors as they begin their new work. I remember back when we first started the Fairfax Baptist Temple that the Lord led Dave and Margaret Abbey to be part of our new church. It was such an encouragement to Mary and me. I highly recommend that every new pastor pray for some couple with a heart for the Lord, for the work, and for him to join his endeavor. All sending pastors need to consider allowing the intern/church planter the freedom to recruit some couples from the church to go with him. We have had anywhere from one to about a dozen families go with one of our church planters.

People will also be needed to help prepare the packets that will be delivered to each door. Much stuffing, sorting, and collating has to be done. You can arrange a special work time for adults or plan a teen activity to help the new church with preparing their literature packets. Some folks can help design the stationary, tracts, flyers, and a church website.

A complete team will be needed the week that the church starts. It is thrilling to be able to take a whole group of people with us to help when we send someone out to start a church. Encourage people to take time off work to go with you. It's key that the sending pastor and the new pastor agree on the date and time to start the church so that they can let people know about it ahead of time. The sending pastor should lead the way, showing his commitment to the new church. This is a great thing in which to involve families, singles, and teen groups. Have people sign up to go, and then arrange for the transportation and lodging. We normally have twenty-five to fifty people who will go with us. Each one pays for his own transportation to the area, as well as lodging, and our church helps with some of the meals and local transportation. It is a great investment for anyone to make!

PARTNERSHIP

The work of giving birth to a new church is a supernatural work. There is nothing easy about it, yet it is not the result of man's endeavors. It is a joint proposition, a partnership with God, the sending church, supporting churches, and the new pastor. God is doing the work. The rest of us are simply working together, relying on Him for the results. *"For of him, and through him, and to him, are all things: to whom be glory forever. Amen"* (Romans 11:36). Praise the Lord for His work and His relationship with us.

THREE

RAISING UP CHURCH PLANTERS

Every time I read the story of Israel's Exodus from Egypt, I am amazed at how little the human heart has changed over these 3,500 years. We are still apt to forget the goodness and blessings of the Lord.

God used Moses to liberate the Israelites from Pharaoh's strong grasp and lead the people to the edge of the Red Sea while Pharaoh chased behind, just to give one more sensational demonstration of His awesome power—the opening of the Red Sea. Over a million Israelites crossed over the sea on dry land. When Pharaoh's army tried to follow, God released the walls of water to drown them. It seems to me that God's miraculous intervention and deliverance would have been hard to forget, but in a matter of weeks or perhaps months, it appears that all was forgotten.

God had been faithfully supplying food for the nation so that no one lacked provision, but notice their "gratefulness" as recorded in the Bible:

> And when the people complained, it displeased the LORD: and the LORD heard it; and his anger was kindled; and the fire of the LORD burnt among them, and consumed them that were in the uttermost parts of the camp. And the people cried unto Moses; and when Moses prayed unto the LORD, the fire was quenched. And he called the name of the place Taberah: because the fire of the LORD burnt among them. And the mixt multitude that was among them fell a lusting: and the children of Israel also wept again, and said, Who shall give us flesh to eat? We remember the fish, which we did eat in Egypt freely; the cucumbers, and the melons, and the leeks, and the onions, and the garlick: But our soul is dried away: there is nothing at all, beside this manna, before our eyes. And the manna was as coriander seed, and the colour thereof as the colour of bdellium.
> —NUMBERS 11:1–7

Let's get the picture of what is happening in this text. Moses was actually going through a congregational crisis, of sorts. There were some difficulties and struggles. The people had been complaining and griping, which in turn stirred up the anger of the Lord, who sent fire to consume many of the people. The mixed multitude with them started lusting. They could almost smell grilled sirloin and fried chicken! They were sick of their steady diet of manna, having eaten it for forty years. Fed up, this mixed multitude decided to take things into their own hands.

Moses felt the burden of all this. He felt oppressed because of all the complaining and griping in his congregation, and he really didn't know what to do. Pastor, have you ever felt the confusion Moses was experiencing? You don't need me to tell you that we're living in difficult days; I think we all realize that. Yet these are glorious days in which to minister in the New Testament church.

The Bible doesn't tell us that Moses spent a lot of time trying on his own to figure out a solution to the problems he faced. It seems that Moses' first thought was to turn to God. Please read the following passage of Scripture to understand Moses' situation and his response, which will bring us to the main point of the chapter:

> THESE ARE GLORIOUS DAYS IN WHICH TO MINISTER IN THE NEW TESTAMENT CHURCH.

And Moses went out, and told the people the words of the Lord, and gathered seventy men of the elders of the people, and set them round about the tabernacle. And the Lord came down in a cloud, and spake unto him, and took of the spirit that was upon him, and gave it unto the seventy elders: and it came to pass, that, when the spirit rested upon them, they prophesied, and did not cease. But there remained two of the men in the camp, the name of the one was Eldad, and the name of the other Medad: and the spirit rested upon them; and they were of them that were written, but went not out unto the tabernacle: and they prophesied in the camp. And there ran a young man, and told Moses, and said, Eldad and Medad do prophesy in the camp. And Joshua the son of Nun, the servant of Moses, one of his young men, answered and said, My lord Moses, forbid them. And Moses said unto him, Enviest thou for my sake? Would God that all the Lord's people were prophets, and that the Lord would put his spirit upon them! And Moses gat him into the camp, he and the elders of Israel.—NUMBERS 11:24–30

So the Lord told Moses to select seventy men to help him better minister to the people. To begin their teaching and training, he took these men away for a few seminars on ministering. All the men came, except for a couple of "rebels" who stayed behind in the camp.

A young man came running to Moses and said, "Moses! Moses! Eldad and Medad are still back home preaching to everyone, and they won't come to attend your seminar. Moses, what should we do about it?"

Joshua spoke up quickly and said, "Yeah, Moses, we've got to do something about these guys. Let's put a stop to it right away!"

That's when Moses responded saying, *"Would God that **all** the Lord's people were prophets, and that the Lord would put his Spirit upon them"* (emphasis added) (Numbers 11:29). Take note of Moses' response because it holds a tremendous lesson for each one of us.

A young couple was saved at our church. They were childless. After a few years of praying, God blessed them with a wonderful baby boy. When the boy was about five years old, the couple came to me and said, "Pastor, we just want you to know that we will not be sending our son to the Fairfax Baptist Temple Academy."

I said, "Well, that's okay. You know it's your prerogative. You do what you think is best."

And they said, "Don't you want to know why?"

"No," I said, "that's your business." (Actually, I did want to know!)

"Well, let us tell you anyway," they continued. "We feel that if we send him to the Fairfax Baptist Temple Academy, he is likely to get called into the ministry. It seems that you all put a lot of pressure on young men to be pastors and missionary-evangelists. We're just not sure that's what we want for our son."

I said, "You've made a good decision then, because there is a conspiracy in our school! It would be a great joy to us if the Lord put all the students attending our academy into the ministry." We would love for all the young men to start churches and for all the young ladies to be preachers' wives or servants in some other capacity. If God doesn't call them, that's fine as well. We are going to train every one of them to be servants for the Lord Jesus Christ and to be open to His perfect will.

I'm with Moses. I really do wish that God would call everyone into the ministry. Now I realize He will not call everyone to a salaried ministry. But ask yourself how many men and boys have been called into the ministry from your church. How many churches have been started from your church? I don't want you to misunderstand my questioning. I'm not asking you to compare your performance with others. I think we all know that is wrong. I'm asking you how great your burden for world evangelism is. It's not a performance thing. It's not a success thing. Our desire should be something akin to Moses' desire, seeing God raise up laborers to do His work. There's a world out there in dire need of the Lord Jesus Christ, but they need someone to go where they are and tell them about Him.

THE HEARTBEAT OF THE CHURCH

The heartbeat of the church should be world evangelism, which is, obviously, the purpose for its existence. I have always believed that every church should have two main goals: 1) to glorify God and 2) to evangelize the world. The Scriptures are very clear on this matter: every church is to have as its primary goal that of glorifying the Lord by starting more churches to reach the lost of this world. Because this is God's purpose for the church, we have no business trying to redefine it. What we need to define is our plan for carrying out the purpose. Pastors, this is our responsibility. The congregation's burden for the world will be no stronger than their pastor's burden.

Biblically, God has only one program to accomplish the task of world evangelism, and that is church planting through the local church. It is the church to which God has promised *"...the gates of hell shall not prevail against it"* (Matthew 16:18). Be careful of para-church organizations seeking your time, attention, and money. Some of them can be very good, but none of them can replace the local church and its ministries.

To keep the program of church planting before your people, I highly recommend having at least a yearly missions conference. (I'll be talking more about that in chapter 11.) I also recommend, Pastor, that you and your wife visit the foreign mission field every year or two. This is how God first spoke to my heart about the need for

> HOW MANY CHURCHES HAVE BEEN STARTED FROM YOUR CHURCH?

world evangelism. Jeremiah recorded in Lamentations 3:51, after God showed him the coming destruction of Judah, *"Mine eye affecteth mine heart."* Your heart and life will be changed after visiting the foreign field.

Clearly then, if you are going to be a reproducing church, if yours is going to be a church that starts other churches, you are going to have to find men who answer the specific call of God to plant churches.

HOW TO RAISE UP MEN

How do you raise up men who desire God's call to ministry? Praying for God to work in the lives of your men is absolutely key. You will find in Matthew 9 a wonderful picture of the Lord's heart. The Bible tells us in verse 36, *"But when he [Jesus] saw the multitudes, he was moved with compassion on them, because they*

fainted, and were scattered abroad, as sheep having no shepherd."
And so, I say we should strive to emulate the Lord.

The first thing I see in this verse is the Lord's compassion.
The Lord had great compassion upon the people: *"When he saw
the multitudes, he was moved with compassion."* In seeing the lost,
we too, should have this compassion, and then we need to teach
our congregations to have this compassion as well.

The second thing I see is the Lord's concern. *"Then saith he
unto his disciples, The harvest truly is plenteous but the labourers
are few"* (Matthew 9:37). The problem is not the harvest; the
problem is the labor shortage. God's answer to the problem is
found verse 38: *"Pray ye therefore the Lord of the harvest, that
he will send forth labourers into his harvest."* How many times
do we neglect this simple command of God? Stop and
think for a moment, as a pastor or a man in the ministry, how
long has it been since you

> THE PROBLEM IS
> NOT THE HARVEST;
> THE PROBLEM IS THE
> LABOR SHORTAGE.

honestly prayed before God, "Lord, please raise up another
missionary-evangelist or pastor from our midst." Maybe the
reason you're not seeing more men called is because it has been
a while since you have prayed this prayer. God's Word says,
"...Ye have not, because ye ask not" (James 4:2). So ask God!

We need to work overtime, laboring in prayer, to get more
laborers into the field that is already ripe unto harvest. Will we
have enough compassion and concern to pray for laborers?

GIVE LOVE

I suggest, while endeavoring to raise up more men for church planting, that you as a pastor love your people and your ministry. Some men and boys may not even consider the call of God because they see how miserable some preachers are and assume that is the best the ministry has to offer. I have always said to preachers that the one thing we cannot afford is the luxury of discouragement or depression. You cannot come into the pulpit and say, "Man alive, I was sure hoping there would be more people here today. I worked hard preparing this message. But (big sigh) I'll go ahead and share it with you anyway."

Don't carry church problems or your own personal problems with you into the pulpit. I hope we all realize that we can't afford to do that. Too much is at stake. The men and boys of our churches need to see us enjoying what we are doing. We must validate to them that it is a wonderful thing to be in the ministry and that it is a great privilege to be the man whom God selects to proclaim His Word! It makes no difference who shows up to hear us or what our difficulties are, we must give ministry our best effort.

Don't make the ministry look like a hardship. Don't slump at the shoulders and be down-in-the-mouth, saying, "Oh well, I could have been a successful business man, but instead I've decided to go ahead and yield to God and go into the ministry." We know that being in the ministry in the perfect will of God is a whole lot better than anything the world has to offer.

Being in the ministry full time has been one of the greatest blessings of my life! It is a privilege to shoulder the burdens and heartaches of people as well as to share in their joys and blessings. The "people business" is the greatest work of all! When I think of the people God gave me the honor of pastoring for thirty-five years, I can say along with the Apostle Paul, "*I thank my God upon every remembrance...*" (Philippians 1:3).

Each of us who is in the ministry, whether full-time or not, should be able to honestly articulate as Paul did, "*And I thank Christ Jesus our Lord, who hath enabled me, for that he counted me faithful, putting me into the ministry*" (1 Timothy 1:12). It is a glorious privilege to be "enabled" by God to be His servant.

A little side note: don't make your wife a widow or your children orphans while you are still alive! It is not a mark of spirituality to say that you don't take a day off or go on vacations. Make sure you give time to your wife and children because, if you don't, you will have no ministry. It is absolutely essential that we minister to our families first and provide for our people a good example of the Christian home.

GIVE ENCOURAGEMENT

In your preaching, challenge people about the plight of a world lost in sin and the great need for laborers to go and win them. World evangelism is for everyone, so we ought to be doing everything possible to encourage our people to reach others for the Lord.

Foster the right environment in your church so that the Holy Spirit has an opportunity to work, calling men and boys as church planting missionary-evangelists or pastors, and encouraging young ladies to be pastors' wives, missionaries' wives, or missionary helpers (as single ladies).

Encouraging young men and ladies into ministry is not without boundaries. We do not generally support single men or single women, especially on the foreign field, because of the temptations that might sully their reputations or otherwise lead to grief and heartache. When considering a single man, I would listen very carefully to determine if he gives credible testimony of a desire for celibacy. I have heard none throughout the years. What I generally hear is that the man is open to marriage but just hasn't found the right young lady.

IT IS A WONDERFUL THING TO BE IN THE MINISTRY.

One of our young men spent some time in a foreign country, intending the experience to be temporary. When he determined that God was indeed calling him to that country, I was very pleased and suggested to him that it was time to find a wife to serve with him. Not so remarkably, it was only a matter of months before God led this young man to a very wonderful woman. They have had a terrific ministry together.

An increasing number of single ladies from within our own congregation and from other churches of like faith and practice are requesting support to go to the mission field. When I started planning the missions program for our church, I had a "no single ladies" policy. I have had to rethink that policy. When a single woman gives testimony of a burden for the foreign field, when that burden is obvious, and when she has immersed herself in the work of her local church—particularly in soulwinning activities—I find it hard to refuse.

The woman needs to prepare herself to be a real help to the missionary-evangelist with whom she will be working. In my view, the ideal undergraduate degree for her would be an education and/or nursing degree with a missions minor. She should have some real world experience as a teacher or nurse before entering the field. While gaining work experience, she could benefit greatly by getting additional Bible training, whether at the Bachelor or Master's degree level. I believe the ideal ministry location is a place with more than one missionary family and well-defined work that the single woman will perform. We do not send a single woman to serve as a nanny/ tutor for the missionary's own children. We presently have three single ladies from our church serving full time in Uganda, Japan, and Brazil. One of these is not in the ideal multiple-missionary family setting, but she is in a place where there are many other Americans. There, the temptations that beset one isolated in a foreign culture are not so great a concern.

Deputation is not easy for a single lady. Many churches are understandably hesitant about supporting a single woman, preferring to support the primary church planter instead. What I have come to realize is that what Paul wrote to Timothy in 2 Timothy 2:4 applies to men and women equally. *"No man that warreth entangleth himself with the affairs of this life; that he may please him who hath chosen him to be a soldier."* And I have seen the truth of what Paul wrote in 1 Corinthians 7:7–8: *"For I would that all men were even as I myself. But every man hath his proper gift of God, one after this manner, and another after that. I say therefore to the unmarried and widows, It is good for them if they abide even as I."* Since the unmarried woman on the mission field is free from the encumbrances of family, she may engage in discipleship, soulwinning, and ministry more fully than the missionary-evangelist's wife who has children to care for.

I would be remiss if I did not add that life on the foreign field, especially in third world countries, is a lonely and solitary life for the unmarried woman. When the missionary-evangelist goes home to wife and family, the single woman goes to her room alone. If we learn anything from Genesis 2, it is that humans need companionship that even intimate, perfect fellowship with God did not satisfy. Adam needed Eve. Not one of

DON'T MAKE YOUR WIFE A WIDOW OR YOUR CHILDREN ORPHANS WHILE YOU ARE STILL ALIVE!

the young women we have sent out prefers her solitary life to the hope of marriage. However, each of them is satisfied to wait patiently on God and to work the work He has set before them while waiting. These are very special women.

At every opportunity, challenge your people to consider occupational ministry. Don't be afraid of interfering with the Holy Spirit's leading. Often we back off and say, "Well, I don't want to say too much. If God doesn't call you, you're not called." That is a truism, but it doesn't mean that God can't use us to help these fellows recognize that God may be at work in their lives.

We all know that the Lord must do the calling and convicting, or the decision will be an emotional one that won't last. But, ask yourself, who called John Mark? Didn't Barnabas urge him along? Who called Timothy, whose only apparent qualification was that he was "well spoken of"? Didn't Paul ask Timothy to help him in his ministry? From reading 1 Timothy 1:18, I deduce that there were "prophesies" that either led Paul to Timothy or revealed that Timothy was to enter the ministry. Whichever is the case, God used others to involve Timothy, the young man who eventually became the pastor of the church at Ephesus.

There are three things that may discourage your people rather than encourage them. First, don't give the impression that preachers are some kind of supernatural Christians, because, the truth of the matter is, we are not. We're made of the same old, fleshly stuff that everyone else is made of. I hope we have learned to say no to the lusts of our flesh more resolutely and more frequently than others, but we are tempted just like everyone else—perhaps even more so. Do you know the stock from which we descend? It's pretty miserable, and apart from Christ, we are hopeless. We are only sinners saved by God's grace. Although our position is high and holy, let us never think that we are. *"Pride goeth before destruction, and an haughty spirit before a fall"* (Proverbs 16:18). Don't become the next tragic story of a fallen "man of the cloth."

Second, don't make the statement, "If you can do anything else, stay out of the ministry." Who in the world ever started that? There is no verse in the Bible to support that position. What do you think the average man is going to surmise when we make that kind of statement? "Well, I've been a successful hamburger flipper at McDonalds, and since I can do that job so well, I guess I can't go into the ministry." We preachers know how to flip hamburgers too! I understand what people mean by that statement, that we know deep within our hearts that our unction is from the Holy Spirit of God, but the average layman may not discern the full meaning. Be careful.

Third, don't make it sound as though the calling is a warm and fuzzy feeling. It is not. The best way to recognize the call, I believe, is the way Spurgeon described it: "An overwhelming desire for the work of the ministry." The Bible says in 1 Timothy 3:1, *"This is a true saying, if a man desire the office of a bishop, he desireth a good work."* We all understand the overwhelming burden, the strong desire that we just can't get off our minds. We must communicate this passion, presenting life in the ministry in such a way that young men listening will desire it too. Being genuinely excited about what you do is what causes others to become interested in doing the same thing.

GIVE TIME

As the Lord Jesus Christ did, I highly recommend that all of us spend time with our men, particularly those men who are called into the ministry. In Mark 3:14 the Bible says, *"And he ordained twelve, that they should be with him, and that he might send them forth to preach."* He ordained them not just to preach; He ordained them to be *"with Him."* "Hey guys, come on with me. Watch me. Do as I do." This is an example of mentoring or discipling. It is investing in the lives of other people.

Pastor, I am sure that you have experienced something similar to what I am about to share with you: I was talking to a neighbor one day. She was having a struggle with her married son, who has three children. His wife had put him out of the home, and it looked as if they were going to divorce. This neighbor looked at me and said, "Bud, I know I should have called you right away, but I know you're so busy, and I didn't want to bother you." Doesn't it just frustrate you when people say that? I think, "That's why I'm here! That's what my life is about and what I love doing! That's what brings joy and excitement to my soul—helping other people!" My time is something I can give to show people I care.

> MY TIME IS SOMETHING I CAN GIVE TO SHOW PEOPLE I CARE.

When working with an intern or encouraging a man from your congregation who believes God is calling him to the ministry, use your experiences to emphasize that ministry is 24/7. Because counseling is a large part of what a pastor does, share with the man how you go about dealing with problems people bring to you. Every man preparing for the ministry needs as much help and training as he can get before he is the one responding to calls for help! Teach your men biblical principles to impart to others in their time of need. All of our hours are God's; let's invest them in building people for the work of the ministry.

GIVE VISION

If you have a church school, make sure it is ministry-oriented. We have dedicated the tenth grade Bible class to world evangelism, and our teacher wrote a text and teacher's guide for the course so that the emphasis and instruction is exactly in line with everything we teach at church about glorifying God and evangelizing the world. Present the needs of the world to your young people as often as you can. Have a strong missions emphasis in chapel. Every time we have a missionary at our church—a minimum of once a month—we invite him to preach in chapel. We've also had missionaries who are passing through stop off and preach in chapel. Have your annual missions conference during the academic school year to involve and influence your young people. Keep in mind that once these young people go off to college, there is a good chance you won't have the opportunity to minister to them again.

In the youth group at church, keep the challenge of ministry before the young people. Instruct them regarding the joys of serving the Lord as a missionary-evangelist or pastor. Remind the minister of youth or youth director that your goal is to get as many of your young people into the ministry as possible. What we are really doing is creating an environment for the Holy Spirit to do as He pleases, not because He needs our help, but because we make yielding their lives priority number one for young people. Make sure that the "heroes" of the youth group are not the sports players but the young people who have yielded their lives for service to our King.

In the children's church, bring ministry work down to their level. Invite different staff members to tell the children what they do to serve the Lord. Let them see and hear missionary-evangelists for themselves. Continually interject missionary stories and interesting anecdotes regarding church life and ministry into their lessons.

With your single adults group, be quick to point out that they are not too old to consider the ministry as a life's work. Remind these young adults that if Moses was eighty and Paul was forty before entering the ministry, they certainly are not too old. Often they focus on their college major or other vocational training and think that they are unqualified to go into the ministry. They may be thinking that they don't want to go back to college for another four years, but more than likely, they could be trained in a much shorter time span right in your own church.

GIVE HONOR

Give honor to invited pastors and missionary-evangelists when they come to speak. Make sure the attitude you convey is not, "Well, we're really busy, but we'll go ahead and give you a minute or two to share how God called you to the ministry and what you've been doing on the mission field for the last twenty years!" Let's make sure we honor them as God's special vessels chosen for His ministry.

Publicly acknowledge students who have been called to minister as church planters or in other capacities. Have a preachers' club or, to include the young ladies as well, a ministry club. Within the ministry club, you might call the men's side Delta Sigma Pi, derived from 1 Corinthians 2:4, *"My speech and my preaching was not with enticing words of man's wisdom, but in demonstration of the Spirit and of power."* Delta Sigma Pi—Demonstration of Spirit and Power. Take time, Pastor, to meet with these young men periodically. Our young men meet with the minister of youth once a week. You can use this as a time to teach them about preparing a message, preaching, or anything else concerning the ministry you care to share. For the young ladies who are open to the Lord's leading into full-time service or marrying a young man called into the full-time Gospel ministry, our desire is to emphasize the importance of the homemaker in God's economy. In Proverbs 31, God gives us the portrait of a Christian wife and mother who is talented and industrious. The ministerial wives (and, during the missions conferences, the missionary wives) meet with these young ladies periodically to encourage them in the many important ways that a wife complements her husband's work in the ministry.

YOUR GOAL IS TO GET AS MANY OF YOUR YOUNG PEOPLE INTO THE MINISTRY AS POSSIBLE.

Something we started doing twice a year is having the young men who believe themselves called to preach meet with a visiting missionary-evangelist before the Wednesday service for a meal and time of sharing. In this informal setting the young men learn to respect the man and have opportunity to hear, in a personal way, how God dealt with him.

Consider teaching a class to the men and boys who have been called, such as a Sunday night Bible institute, to share with them some practical aspects of the ministry.

GIVE OPPORTUNITY

Plan to have regular teen and adult missions trips. We have had the joy of taking adults and teens to the foreign field and seeing some of them called into the ministry. We have also taken teens, singles, and couples with us to start churches in the United States, and the Lord has wonderfully blessed. Many of these people have been called into the ministry as well. Your people's hearts will be affected and their lives changed as they see the ministry first hand.

GIVE GOD'S WORD

When we go out to start a church, we pass out "Gospel Blitz" bags containing a Gospel of John and Romans or a beautifully printed sermon booklet, a Gospel tract, and a letter from the pastor inviting them to come, which includes the time and place of the first service. We usually pass out over twenty thousand of these at a cost of about $6,500 each time we start a church.

After years of doing this blitzing to get new churches started, I thought, "We don't have to start a church to distribute door hangers." So, when we moved to our new facilities, we printed up a Gospel of John and Romans with a beautiful full-color cover. On the inside cover we put an invitation, a picture of our family, and some information about our church. Then we passed out 100,000 of these to our neighbors, just to get the word out that we were relocating. Now every month, we have what we call a "Gospel Blitz," where the young and old alike can get a burden for witnessing. This activity involves going to doors throughout the area and placing plastic door-hanger bags filled with information about the church; a salvation tract; information about upcoming events like Vacation Bible School, missions conference, revival, a particular sermon title or series, etc.; a personal letter from the pastor inviting them to visit; and one of the booklets I wrote like *How to Deal with How You Feel,* or *When You Feel Out of Love with Your Spouse.* (Leafleting is a constitutionally protected practice. It is not soliciting. However, you need to honor "no trespassing" signs.) We have many different services and activities to which we can invite the community: Thanksgiving service, December activities, an upcoming seminar, Patriot's Day remembrance service where we honor the first-responder community, Easter service, Missions Conference, July 4th Celebration Service, etc. Having many different services and activities provides opportunities for outreach. I simply encourage you to consider this approach when starting churches and expanding the outreach of your own church.

We have had people saved and baptized as a result of the door hangers. They don't come in droves by any means. But, in my opinion, it is kind of like "market place" preaching: you get the Word out and trust God's promise that it will not return void. I learned years ago, that people aren't as quick to throw away a Bible or a portion of the Bible, so it serves as a constant reminder. I was impressed once when the literature left on the door of a Jewish lady was returned to us. Her note said that she did not want the material but could not throw away things with

God's name. We wrote back, refunding her postage. (If only everyone had such respect for God's Word and name!)

GIVE KNOWLEDGE

Provide an internship program for every man and boy called to the ministry from your church. At Fairfax Baptist Temple, we offer to every man called into the ministry the opportunity to serve an internship at our church. This is something I believe to be vitally important. To young men, we offer this program during the summers between college academic years and after they graduate.

Our adult internship is a minimum of one year. Interns have to agree to stay from one to three years. We pay them a livable salary, but not so much that they get too comfortable. During the term of internship, we teach them as many phases of the ministry as we can by rotating them through our ministerial staff so they see the different things we do and learn how to do them. They are allowed to preach in church and chapel from time to time. We also include them in an occasional staff meeting and deacons meeting. But we don't use them as full-time teachers or janitors or bus workers.

We teach all of our interns the right philosophy regarding world evangelism. Keep in mind, most missionary-evangelists, as well as many churches, don't have the broad view of world evangelism that God wants them to have. For this reason, we indoctrinate them in church planting philosophy and methodology. By the way, for those of you who are interested, we have an example of our internship plan. If you get ready to start one, contact us and we'd be more than happy to let you have a copy of what we do at our church.

GIVE GOD ALL THE GLORY

Being a church planter is a gift of God's grace, nothing else. It is the Lord who does the calling, so let us be looking for faithful men and boys in whom we can invest our time. *"The things that thou hast heard of me among many witnesses, the same commit thou to faithful men, who shall be able to teach others also"* (2 Timothy 2:2).

Gentlemen, it is the greatest blessing and the most exciting thing in the world to see some of your men and ladies surrender to the ministry. I don't mind telling you, of all the men we have had called to the ministry, my greatest joy is that God called our own son, Troy, to be a pastor. After seventeen years of working with me on staff as pastor of our Spanish ministry, he now pastors the Fairfax Baptist Temple.

What a great and wonderful privilege it is to have God at work calling and putting men and women into the ministry from the church you pastor. Would to God that the Lord would make all His people prophets and put His Spirit upon them. Pastor, even now, as you begin praying that God would raise up men from your congregation, give Him all the glory for what He will do.

FOUR

PRELIMINARY
CONSIDERATIONS

My foundational premise is that the desire of the pastor's heart is to faithfully perform his office as pastor of a local New Testament church. The motivating force driving this desire is love—love for God, love for the flock, and love for the lost of the world. Faithfulness in discharging all of the duties of this office is nothing more and nothing less than patterning his ministry after Jesus Christ's. I believe that the pattern Jesus gave us is world evangelism through church planting.

Most Bible-believing, Bible-preaching pastors and their congregations readily give mental assent to the fact that the Bible teaches world evangelism. Faithfulness to God, however, requires more than mere assent. Faithfulness requires each one of us to pray for and desire the heart of Christ—a heart for the lost. I am not talking about simply being knowledgeable about the need for world evangelism through church planting; I am talking about seeing the world through Jesus' eyes. As pastors, we must see the need—literally see it.

Allow me to reiterate my testimony: As the result of the first trip Mary and I made to the mission field, the Spirit of God broke my heart. I understood in a new and profound way the emotion of Jeremiah as the same Spirit moved him to record in Lamentations, *"Mine eye affecteth mine heart…"* (3:51). There is a similar passage, describing how the eye affects the heart in Matthew 9:35–38. A portion of that passage reads, *"But when he* [Jesus] *saw the multitudes, he was moved with compassion…."* In other words, His eye affected His heart. *"Then saith he unto his disciples… Pray ye therefore the Lord of the harvest, that he will send forth labourers…."* We, and the men called as pastors or church planting evangelists (missionaries), are an answer to those prayers.

> WE STAND APPROVED BEFORE GOD ON THE BASIS OF OUR CONSISTENCY AND STEADFASTNESS TO THE WORK AND THE PURITY OF OUR HEARTS.

Our approval before God as a pastor does not depend on the results of our "performance." God alone is responsible for the results. We stand approved before God on the basis of our consistency and steadfastness to the work and the purity of our hearts—doing the work with a proper motivation, that His name may be lifted up, not ours. Yet we do desire to see fruit and much fruit from our labor. In the still of the evening, you may find yourself meditating, as I have, on Isaiah 5:4: *"What could have been done more to my vineyard, that I have not done in it? Wherefore, when I looked that it should bring forth grapes, brought it forth wild grapes?"* God has given me everything that I need to accomplish His mission, fulfilling the Great Commission. The question that remains is whether I, as a pastor, have done all that I can.

In dealing with Israel and Judah, God asks the rhetorical question, "What could have been done more to my vineyard, that I have not done in it?" He's not really expecting an answer. God is about to pronounce judgment upon Israel and Judah, and He wants to show His justification for what He is about to do to them for their injustice. He laments, "I have sown all these wonderful grapes in my beloved vineyard (Israel). I've done everything for you: I've been your God. I've been your loving Father, your Protector, your Provider. Now tell me what could I have done more?" No one could say that He hadn't been fair. So He metes out six different judgments upon Israel.

One point for consideration is that wherever we go to do God's bidding, the harvest field or vineyard is His. He says in verse 7, *"For the vineyard of the Lord of hosts is the house of Israel, and the men of Judah his pleasant plant: and he looked for judgment, but behold oppression; for righteousness, but behold a cry."* It is His vineyard.

Another point to consider: God takes account of His vineyard. Since He does, we need to think about how we can cultivate this vineyard or harvest field where He has placed us. How can we carry out this God-given responsibility? How can we best be used to serve our wonderful Saviour? As we journey through this life, it is good to continually ask ourselves what could have been done more to His vineyard? In other words, ask yourself, "Have I done my best for Jesus?" We need to make sure that we are doing the will and work of our Lord.

In the letter from Jesus Christ to the church at Ephesus set out in Revelation 2:4, Jesus states that He knows the work of that local church, that they have labored and not fainted. Jesus continues saying, *"Nevertheless I have somewhat against thee, because thou hast left thy first love."* Exactly what this first love is has been the topic of much discussion.

I believe that the first love of every pastor must be the same as the first love of our Saviour. What is the first love of our Lord? I think we find the answer in Luke 19:10 (and elsewhere): *"For the Son of man is come to seek and to save that which was lost."* What is true for a pastor is true of every Christian. If your heart is right, if your desire is the first love of our King, if your desire is God's desire, you will have a heart for worldwide church planting missions.

Responding to a lawyer who, intent upon trapping Jesus, asked Him which is the greatest commandment, Jesus gave what was probably a completely unanticipated response.

> *Jesus said unto him, Thou shalt love the Lord thy God with all thy heart, and with all thy soul, and with all thy mind. This is the first and great commandment. And the second is like unto it, Thou shalt love thy neighbour as thyself.*—MATTHEW 22:37–39

If you have such a heart, you will be faithful and obedient to demonstrate your love for your Saviour (John 14:15). Jesus Christ's love for you and your love for Him inspirit your compassion for people and your passion to act. Pastor, this heart to love God and to love the people He loves is the key for faithfulness in the performance of your office. If you will be faithful to your office, you will count the cost of cultivating His "vineyard" and plan wisely to perform this stewardship.

THE RIGHT MAN FOR THE JOB

Starting churches is not for sissies. That doesn't sound real theological; nevertheless, it is biblically true. It is vitally important that the man the church is sending out is of the conviction that he is the man for the job because it is not going to be easy. He had better know who he is and who God is and make sure of his calling. Church planting is difficult work. The devil doesn't like it.

God wants some men to take over existing churches. We do have tens of thousands of Bible-believing, Bible-preaching churches around the country. Pastors die, pastors change, pastors quit, pastors disqualify themselves, so there are always existing churches looking for a pastor to lead them.

Before you embark on the work of planting a new church, make sure you are not one of those men that God wants to use to take over an existing church (You also need to make sure that your gift is that of pastor as opposed to missionary-evangelist). It takes a different disposition in a man to start a church than to take over an existing one. You need to think all this through. I've had to analyze these things myself. I am not saying that one person is more spiritual than another or this way is better than that. God is God, and you cannot put Him in a box. You have to be willing to submit to His will.

Mary and I moved to Fairfax years ago to plant a new church. For a few weeks before we started our church, we visited an independent, fundamental Baptist church pastored by Mary's former youth director. We were thrilled to see this couple again, and they were glad to see us. The pastor asked all first-time visitors to introduce themselves, and we did. Right after the service, the man sitting next to me introduced himself and told me he was also a first time visitor. He invited us to his home and said, "It just so happens that I represent about twenty or so families that are looking for a pastor to start a new church."

I thought, "I'm a new pastor starting a new church. I just moved to the area. I came into a friend's church for the first time and sat down next to a man who is also there for the first time and happens to be looking for a pastor to start a church. I can't believe how good God is!" Doesn't that sound like the will of God to you?

He said to me, "Would you mind meeting the other families?"

I said, "I would love to!" So he set up a meeting in his home the next weekend. As we gathered there in his living room, they began sharing testimonies around the room. About the time they got half way around, something started clicking in my mind, and it didn't sound good. I could tell just by listening to them that these people were not going to follow me as their pastor. In fact, they were not going to follow any pastor.

By the time they got around to me I said, "Thanks, but no thanks. I don't think you really want me to be your pastor."

This man handed me a fifty-dollar bill and said, "We believe in taking care of our pastor." (That fifty dollars in 1970 is equivalent to hundreds of dollars today!) Tell me that's not music to a new college graduate's ears!

The problem is they were not looking for a pastor; they were looking for a preacher. They did end up starting a church within a month or so of us, and in their first year they bought property and put up a church building. We used to drive by and read the sign where the pastor's name was displayed. In four years' time they had four different pastors!

I couldn't have created the circumstances of that story if I had tried. The details seemed to work out miraculously, but you must realize the devil can set up circumstances. If you are looking for good things to happen, he can make good things happen. That's why you don't discern the will of God by circumstances alone. I don't know how He did it, but the Lord

HAPPY PASTORS SELDOM LEAVE HAPPY CHURCHES

gave me enough wisdom even then to discern that this situation wasn't for me. Man of God, pray for God's wisdom, and don't let circumstances deter you from doing the will of God.

I think most would understand this scenario: A man finishes school and embarks on the difficult task of starting a church. He sees this beautiful church building gracefully situated on a lovely hillside, it's steeple reaching toward Heaven. Knowing this place is already established with finances, buildings, and a membership, he feels a tug. But taking an existing work is not always the best thing. Generally, though not invariably, pastors don't leave good churches. Happy pastors seldom leave happy churches (I am one of the exceptions)!

It is true that taking over an existing church is much easier early on. You have instant people, instant finances, and often, existing church buildings. There are some immediate advantages to be gained. And an existing church, one that is truly looking for a pastor to lead them in the righteousness of God, can be a wonderful situation for the man God sends. But do not ignore the fact that you will be walking into a group of people that already have an established way of doing things. There are probably deacons, committees, and programs that may not fit your ministry plan and philosophies. There will be budgets, debts, and priorities that you did not establish. Every existing church already has a personality and a history, and the most recent history of that church may be a sense of failure, frustration, or disappointment. When you take over a church, there is probably some expectation that you will go with the flow—a "this is the way *we* do it" mentality. It's not that your way is necessarily a whole lot better than everyone else's, it's just that you can live with your way, and you may be blindsided by theirs. In an existing church, there may be some resistance to change. (Did I say *may* be?) Be prepared for some of the people to just walk away.

Shortly after graduating from Bible college, I confirmed in my own mind that taking over an existing church was not for me. In 1970, when I graduated from Bible college, I went out with an instrumental music ensemble as the preacher. That summer we traveled to about eighty-five churches in the Mid-West. While the team of five students was practicing, I would go talk to the pastor. I would ask him how long he had been there, how the work was going, and what advice he could offer a new church planter. Time after time, I heard similar stories from pastors who had taken over existing works but had not realized when they started that there were issues with controlling families. Having been at their churches for several years, some of those pastors were thinking about leaving to go to another existing work, though I don't know why they expected the next one to be any different. I realized I didn't want that.

That said, there are some wonderful churches furthering world evangelism through church planting that were existing works taken over by men whom God had prepared for those pulpits. I only mention all of this to say that while there may be immediate benefits to an existing work, in the long run, you may still be trying to work out problems that are not yours.

It's not that you won't have problems when you start a new church; it's just that you know what they are. You eliminate the element of surprise. You should never try to run from problems, but what makes them much more difficult to handle is not being able to identify the problem or not knowing the extent of the problem.

When you start a church, it has no history or preexisting organizational personality. You get to establish these things. I need to add one word of caution. Even when you start a church, you need to be very careful because everything you do for the first time is a precedent. (If you don't like to stay up past midnight for watch night services on New Year's Eve, don't have one!)

When you start your own church, make the pulpit ministry a priority. If there was ever a time that the pulpit ministry should be given prominence, it is today when so many churches have services to entertain, throwing in a little sermonette on the side. You set the precedent on how things are done when you start a new church. In my opinion, laying this foundation is key.

You set the direction as to where the church is headed (that, by the way, is called leadership) rather than try to turn around a church that may be headed down the wrong path. You establish the biblical doctrine and music philosophy. You establish leadership standards. You establish priorities.

You set the separation standards—both personal and ecclesiastical. Those two standards can make or break you and your church as fast as anything I know. If you go ahead and dabble in a little bit of worldliness, I promise you will open the floodgates to a deluge. If you mess around with a little bit of worldly "Christian" music (an oxymoron, I know; I mean to indicate that there is nothing God honoring about it) and other forms of compromise, it won't take long before they flood in and inundate your church.

You establish the missions philosophy and program. You recommend the budget which sets the tone financially. If you completely turn financial responsibility over to someone else such as a treasurer or deacons, you misunderstand the role of biblical leadership in the church. It is good for someone else to do the work, but you should take the lead.

One aspect of church leadership is a source of terror for most new pastors—deacons and deacons meetings. When I started Fairfax Baptist Temple, I had already heard about the potential problems a pastor could have with deacons, and personally, I was a little nervous! But our deacons turned out to be my best friends and were some of the greatest people in the world with whom to work! By the way, you don't have to have deacons meetings or church business meetings every month. Wait until you have something to talk about. At

MAKE THE PULPIT MINISTRY A PRIORITY.

Fairfax Baptist Temple, we have one annual business meeting and five or six deacons meetings a year. It is important that you set the agenda, and that you lead those meetings.

Taking a biblical stand for the Lord and providing strong leadership is harder for young pastors today than it was when I started. Young men, make sure you are the right man for the job and that you are standing on the right position and focusing on the right thing.

WHERE TO START A CHURCH

As the sending pastor one of your concerns is to evangelize the region in which you are located. Paul wrote to his young preacher boy in 2 Timothy 4:5, *"But watch thou in all things, endure afflictions, **do the work of an evangelist**, make full proof of thy ministry"* (emphasis mine). Every local church has a responsibility to evangelize the area of its influence and to send out men to extend that reach.

The sending pastor and the new church pastor must work together and seek agreement, never communicating any disagreement to the church. I don't require any of our ministerial staff members to believe exactly as I do on everything. I don't expect that of my wife! The same is true with pastors working together to start a church. There are some essential things, however, about which you should be in agreement. You need to work things out so that together, as one, you can present the burden to start a new church. The sending pastor must have total peace about the direction the new church planter is headed.

GOD MUST BE THE ONE WHO LEADS THE CHURCH.

God must be the one who leads the church and the pastor. New pastor, ask God for a genuine burden for a particular city or people. I say that because there are all kinds of places in the United States, and even more around the world, in which to start a church.

As a pastor just starting out, you should be looking for a place where you will not be competing with another man who is preaching sound doctrine. Discern an area where there is a *genuine* need. Just because a pastor in a potential area differs from you about some point of separation doesn't mean you should strike out to start a new church there. Churches are needed where people do not have an opportunity to be members of a good, Bible-believing, Bible-preaching church.

Consider who you are as a church planter and where you would be comfortable ministering. You may be thinking about somewhere in the United States or somewhere overseas. Ultimately, God has to be the one who leads you in this decision. But if you do not already have a clear direction from the Lord, these are questions to consider: Where have you lived most of your life? Do you have any particular regional likes or dislikes? Do you love or hate the mountains? What about the ocean? Do you like the city or the country? Try to discern where you think you might fit in. Once I planted six tomato plants in my back yard and reaped a grand total of three tomatoes. I was so proud of them! What am I saying? Since I know nothing about rural life, pastoring in a farming community would probably not have been a good idea for me!

Some people ask me how I can stand the Washington D.C. metro area with all the traffic. I love it! Think of all those prospects! We started one church in Missouri, and we went to every single house in town. Both of them! No, really, there were about 7,000, and we went to all of them. I prefer an area where there are many people, but some don't.

I've heard some people say that you ought to be careful about telling the Lord what you don't like, but I think that they don't understand God. He made you the way you are with the background you have to do the work He wants you to do. It is vital to be absolutely surrendered to His direction regardless of your preferences, but God does often guide through preferences He has given. Some of these aspects of your background and upbringing may influence your decision:

EDUCATIONAL BACKGROUND

I am totally convinced that God has a place for you regardless of your educational background. There is no premium on ignorance; I don't mean to imply that. But at the same time, you don't need a Ph.D. to go into a country town (or even a city) and tell people about Jesus Christ. There is a prepared place for a prepared man.

PREDILECTION

Psalm 37:4 says, *"Delight thyself also in the Lord; and he shall give thee the desires of thine heart."* There needs to be a match between the church planter and the area in which he plans to start a church. The sending pastor and church cannot force this match. I think the two pastors ought to work together on it, but neither should force it. God's will must be done.

LARGER VS. SMALLER COMMUNITIES

Find out the population of the city and the outlying areas. Personally, I prefer densely populated areas. Unless God has already shown you His perfect will for your life, consider that Paul always went to major cities to start a church (e.g., Corinth, Ephesus, Philippi). I highly recommend doing the same. Start with a large metropolitan area, a place where there are masses of people. That seemed to be Paul's principle for church planting.

HOMETOWN AREA

I would be slow to consider going to an established small town that is not your hometown. You may just wind up spending the first ten years trying to gain acceptance from the town's people. This caution applies regionally as well. There is an old joke about a man spoken of as an outsider in a New England community—after he had lived there thirty years! If you have a heavy regional accent—or don't—it may be the difference between being accepted or not.

NEEDY AREAS

Consider some areas where the sending pastor knows of needs. He could probably tell you of areas within his own state that could use a good church. Use the internet to look at the directories of communities to see what churches are already there.

SURROUNDING AREAS

You may want to contact pastors in the wider surrounding area to get their thoughts. Reassure them that you don't want to be very close to their churches. When one of our fellows did this, he found that an existing church had already purchased land right where he was thinking about locating. Consequently, he went to another town.

ETHNICITY

Look at the ethnic makeup of the town to make sure you are suitable. I don't say that to look down my nose at anybody by any means, but if I plan to start a church in America, I'm not going to move into densely ethnic areas that are different from mine, unless God has burdened me for those people. I'll just end up getting frustrated, they'll get frustrated, and we won't get anywhere.

DEMOGRAPHICS

Consider the demographics of an area. How many other good Bible-believing, Bible-preaching churches are in the area you are considering? In my opinion, if there are good churches teaching sound doctrine and working effectively to bring the clear message of salvation by grace through faith in Jesus Christ alone and if the area is being effectively evangelized, then there is no reason for you as a sending pastor or as a new church planter to place yourself into competition. The real question is this: Is the Gospel being preached? If the Gospel is being preached, I'm glad it's getting done. I may not agree with everything another pastor stands for, but I'm grateful that the Word of God is going out there. So find out how many other good churches—just starting or in existence—are teaching sound doctrine in the area.

SUB-CULTURES

What is the major industry of the town? Is it the home of the auto industry or perhaps carpet mills? Many of the coastal towns in Louisiana, Texas, and California have huge oil refineries, which give rise to a culture all their own. What is the political climate of the town? Is it a blue town or red one? You'll want to have an idea of the prevailing political trend. Are there colleges in town or a military installation? Maybe the area is all farming, where generations of families have lived for a long time. Perhaps it is largely made up of professional people. There are cultures and sub-cultures that are worth finding out about before you make a decision on where to start a church.

After you get a list together, drive to one of the areas you are considering and look around. Look at the people and get a feel for the area. When we moved to Northern Virginia to start a church, I didn't know exactly where it was going to be. I thought about one place, but after looking, I realized that it was 99 percent developed. I wasn't aware of property anywhere. So I started looking in other areas. I went to the police station and the chamber of commerce and talked to people to get a feel for what the areas were like. I looked for new development because I didn't want to get into an established area. I wanted to locate where the growth of the city was going, where new people were moving in. You might want to see where the interstate is or where planners are proposing major highways that would open up the area for development of new communities.

When you have the city in mind where you are going to start, take your map and pinpoint where the existing good churches are. Then look to see which side of the city may still need a church. Ask about the sizes of the churches (not that it matters to the Lord). I started right between two established churches. They were both dead, spiritually. Neither one was soulwinning, and consequently, they were not growing.

LEGAL REQUIREMENTS
SOCIAL SECURITY

Generally, the first legal consideration a church planter has is whether to opt out of the self-employment tax, which is tantamount to a decision about whether to stay in Social Security or not. The Social Security Administration has set down the rules regarding the self-employment tax for ministers. In their handbook, paragraph 1130.3 asks, "Is an exemption available? Ministers, members, or practitioners who are conscientiously opposed to, or because of religious principles are opposed to the acceptance of benefits based on their earnings from these services, may elect to be exempt from coverage by applying to

IRS for an irrevocable exemption." (See also IRS Publication 517.)
Keep in mind that applying for this exemption is not necessarily
the same as determining whether you legally qualify to be
exempt from paying self-employment tax.

"An exemption is obtained by the timely filing with IRS of
Form 4361 *Application for Exemption from Self-employment Tax*
for use by ministers, members of religious orders, and Christian
Science Practitioners." It makes no difference what others
are doing—you must decide what is right for you. Read the
certification carefully:

> I certify that I am conscientiously opposed to, or
> because of my religious principles I am opposed to, the
> acceptance (for services I perform as a minister, member
> of a religious order not under a vow of poverty, or a
> Christian Science practitioner) of any public insurance
> that makes payments in the event of death, disability, old
> age, or retirement; or that makes payments toward the cost
> of, or provides services for, medical care. (Public insurance
> includes insurance systems established by the Social
> Security Act.)
>
> I certify that as a duly ordained, commissioned, or
> licensed minister of a church or a member of a religious
> order not under a vow of poverty, I have informed the
> ordaining, commissioning, or licensing body of my church
> or order that I am conscientiously opposed to, or because
> of religious principles, I am opposed to the acceptance (for
> services I perform as a minister or as a member of a religious
> order) of any public insurance that makes payments in the
> event of death, disability, old age, or retirement; or that

makes payments toward the cost of, or provides services for, medical care, including the benefits of any insurance system established by the Social Security Act.

I certify that I have never filed Form 2031 to revoke a previous exemption from social security coverage on earnings as a minister, member of a religious order not under a vow of poverty, or a Christian Science practitioner.

I request to be exempted from paying self-employment tax on my earnings from services as a minister, member of a religious order not under a vow of poverty, or a Christian Science practitioner, under section 1402(e) of the Internal Revenue Code. I understand that the exemption, if granted, will apply only to these earnings. Under penalties of perjury, I declare that I have examined this application and to the best of my knowledge and belief, it is true and correct.

Clearly, this decision is not to be based on finances but exclusively on your understanding of God's Word concerning how a minister of the Gospel is to be recompensed. Do you have a biblical conviction opposing the government's taxing you and then later providing you with benefits out of your earnings from the church? Personally, I don't like the idea of receiving government benefits from my labor for God. As I read my Bible, there is a definite distinction about the things of God and the things of man. The church and its ministers belong to God. I *"render to Caesar the things that are Caesar's, and to God the things that are God's"* (Mark 12:17). The church is all God's. However, I know other good men of God who look at it differently. You have to decide what you believe.

If you do choose to opt out, do so in a timely manner—at the time of this writing, the Social Security Administration gives two years after ordination to file an exemption—and make sure you are disciplined to plan ahead and save enough money to provide for your financial future what Social Security would have provided had you remained in the program.

There are essentially four things that Social Security provides for you: 1) Some income when you are older, 2) Disability insurance for you now, 3) A very small death benefit (wouldn't you be disappointed if you died and didn't get any benefit from that?), 4) Health insurance when you take on emeritus status (that sounds better than "when you get old").

If you do opt out or even if you don't, you would be wise to start setting aside money for retirement or any ministry change that you may experience later. At minimum, you should start an IRA *yesterday*. The next thing I suggest you do is purchase a disability insurance policy and a life insurance policy. Life insurance, like savings, is wise whether you opt out of Social Security or not. Usually, term insurance is the best and least expensive way to go. It's *insurance*, not an investment. The younger you are and the more children you have at home, the higher your benefits should be. Your church may be able to help you with these three things since they will not be paying the government their share of your social security. As you get your finances in order, be sure to put all your legal papers in a safe place for your permanent file.

INCORPORATION

Check on the legal requirements for establishing a church in a specific area (including the federal tax-exempt requirements and any state-specific incorporating requirements, etc.). For example, in Virginia, a church must have court appointed trustees (though the law is changing to allow for church incorporation). In Kentucky "any person who displays, handles or uses any kind of reptile in connection with any religious service or gathering shall be fined not less than $50 nor more than $100." Virginia has no such limitation!

ZONING LAWS

Check on zoning laws that pertain to churches. Some areas have specific laws regarding what kind of buildings they can meet in and where they can meet. Some require a minimum amount of property. In Fairfax County it is against the law to have a church in your house. In Virginia, a church can build in a light industrial area without special permission. Because zoning is the business of local government, the rules can vary from county to county or town to town within the same state. So you have to be knowledgeable about the laws and ordinances in your specific area.

BORROWING BRAINS

There are three people you as a new pastor should get to know as soon as possible. These are people with whom you want to develop a good relationship—a friendship. Immediately upon arriving in town, you would be prudent to find a good attorney. Ask a nearby pastor who he might recommend. It is a plus to have an attorney who is already familiar with 501(c)(3) (tax-exempt) organizations. If you ask a lawyer a question to which he has no answer, he will agree to do the work for you; then he will research it and charge you for his time. It might be quicker and less expensive to hire someone who already knows the special case.

A banker and a CPA are the other friends you want to make. You should try to find them as quickly as you can. Call for an appointment; then go introduce yourself. Explain what you are doing, and tell them that you would like to draw from their wisdom. As soon as you tell them they are wise, their ears will perk up!

When we were going into a bond program for our first building, I went to a bank, sat down in the banker's office, and said, "We have started a church and want to build a building, and I don't really have a clue how to go about it financially. Would you mind helping me with that?" The banker was delighted to share what he knew about bonds, bank financing, and the steps I needed to take. As Dr. Bob Jones Sr. said, "If you don't have brains, borrow them!" By the way, when preparing to build, be sure to get informed legal counsel if you are considering bonds because the laws have tightened considerably. You do not want to sell bonds in a manner contrary to securities laws. Also, some banks may require that you agree to accept offerings by automatic withdrawal as a condition of the loan.

A little while back I saw a banker whom I had met about twenty-five years ago. We recognized each other immediately and started talking. Now he is president of one of the banks and has told us for years that if we ever needed anything, he would be more than happy to help. It could be to your advantage to establish a personal relationship with these three professionals as soon as possible. You might consider taking them out to lunch. (Sometimes it's a whole lot cheaper to buy a man's lunch than to hear his stopwatch start ticking when you call him on the phone!)

CHURCH CONSTITUTION

The wise sending pastor will require the church planter to make up his church constitution *prior* to his commissioning. Because the sending church wants to reproduce "after its own kind," it is important for the sending church to know the new pastor's doctrinal beliefs, church policies, government, and leadership requirements and responsibilities. When we send fellows out from Fairfax Baptist Temple to start churches, we are basically looking to start another Fairfax Baptist Temple. It's not that we think we have the only way, but we expect something fairly similar to what we are doing as fundamental, independent Baptists. We're not interested in starting community churches or Bible churches, United Methodist or Pentecostal churches, just as those churches don't want the men they send out to start Baptist churches.

Having the constitution written out will allow the two pastors to discuss any differences. They do not have to be in total agreement on everything, but there should at least be a mutual understanding. God doesn't have just one mold. But the sending pastor wants to understand what the new pastor might plan to do differently. He may try to do something he has seen somewhere else without realizing that he is falling into a trap. It might help the new pastor to scrutinize the sending church's constitution and ask any questions he may have.

New Church Planter, you may take the doctrinal portion
of the new church's constitution directly from the written
doctrinal position you presented at your ordination. (You do
not have to rewrite the entire Bible for this!) I also recommend
that you have a small tract printed that is just the doctrinal
statement of your constitution. Many people coming to your
church for the first time will ask for a copy of your doctrine,
and having a tract is handier than giving out a copy of the entire
constitution. It would also be good idea to put your doctrinal
statement on your website.

Your constitution should be the paradigm of how
your church will be administered and what it believes. Most
constitutions include the articles of faith, the course of action
for joining or leaving the church, the biblical requirements
and responsibilities of the pastor and deacons, a few specifics
regarding how and when business meetings are conducted,
the percentage that constitutes a quorum, the procedure to
amend the constitution, and the steps to dissolve (God forbid)
the church. Also, consider including something about how to
handle finances, salaries, and pastoral succession.

Seek the advice of a good lawyer, and find out the laws
of incorporation in your state because the laws differ in each
state. Then work with the sending church to ensure that the
wording in your church constitution is biblically oriented. Legal
ways do not always jibe with biblical ways, but you can take a
legal principle and word it in such a way that you do not have to
violate your conscience.

Note: I would not pastor a church where the constitution
did not reserve the pastor the role of moderator of all business

meetings. The issue is preservation of the God-ordained leadership role, for the sake of the church.

In addition, keep your constitution brief and to the point, and be careful that you don't tie the pastor's hands. When I first started Fairfax Baptist Temple, a nearby church invited me to a preachers' fellowship. They were having a church organizational meeting that Sunday, and they asked us (the preachers) to examine their constitution, which was lengthy (thirty-four pages) and very specific in what the pastor could and could not do. More than likely, the longer the constitution is, the more tightly the pastor's hands will be tied. Keep in mind that the pastor is the shepherd of the flock. He leads. He does not look back and ask the sheep where they want to go next. This leadership role should not be subverted by the church constitution.

Stewarding God's "vineyard" is a solemn responsibility. Ask God for His wisdom in all these matters concerning this stewardship, and seek His will in every detail that you might faithfully perform the task God has entrusted to you.

KEY CONVICTIONS

I thrill to see young men and women who have been moved by the Holy Spirit of God to enter His ministry as a full-time passion. Our churches should always be like a boot camp for God's people, where the Holy Spirit is moving upon the lives of every church member to prepare each one for the work of the ministry. This chapter is devoted to a vital aspect of preparation—developing what I believe to be key convictions for the men whom God has called to serve Him as church planters, convictions that I believe to be necessary to every man of God who desires that God would freely work in and through him. I present these convictions as the montage that constitutes the backbone of a church planter. My prayer is that these rudiments will serve as lampposts along your journey of ministering and act as a guardrail along the straight and narrow way that God has called each church planter to walk.

The Apostle Paul seems to have sensed that he was coming to the end of his life. In Acts 20:25–32, he is telling the elders of Ephesus that, while he probably would not return to the eastern reaches of the Roman Empire (though he did), he had done all that he could to bring the hope of salvation to those people, in that he had confronted every man with his need for the Saviour.

> *And now, behold, I know that ye all, among whom I have gone preaching the kingdom of God, shall see my face no more. Wherefore I take you to record this day, that I am pure from the blood of all men. For I have not shunned to declare unto you all the counsel of God.*
> —ACTS 20:25–27

The apostle's exhortation was intended to strengthen the elders against the persecution that was certain to follow.

> *Take heed therefore unto yourselves, and to all the flock, over the which the Holy Ghost hath made your overseers, to feed the church of God, which he hath purchased with his own blood. For I know this, that after my departing shall grievous wolves enter in among you, not sparing the flock. Also of your own selves shall men arise, speaking perverse things, to draw away disciples after them. Therefore watch, and remember, that by the space of three years I ceased not to warn every one night and day with tears. And now, brethren, I commend you to God, and to the word of his grace, which is able to build you up, and to give you an inheritance among all them which are sanctified.*—ACTS 20:28–32

Keep in mind that the devil does not celebrate when a church is started. New Church Planter, he is devising right now how he might destroy you before you ever get started. Seasoned Ministers, he is waiting for you to let down your guard so that he can slither through the small crack you left unnoticed. Neither of you is as seasoned as your enemy. He has had over 6,000 years of experience in messing up God's work. If you are looking for a lifetime of ease, the pastorate is not a vocation you should consider because it is requires battling a formidable enemy.

The Bible tells us in 2 Timothy 2:4 that *"No man that warreth entangleth himself with the affairs of this life; that he may please him who hath chosen him to be a soldier."* I remind us that the most important thing any man of God has on his agenda each day is to walk with God. With a million distractions in the world, each vying for our time, it is imperative that we set aside time to talk to God in prayer and allow Him to speak to us through His Word. The psalmist said, *"O how love I thy law! It is my meditation all the day"* (Psalm 119:97). Whether a man is serving on the mission field or in the

> THE MOST IMPORTANT THING ANY MAN OF GOD HAS ON HIS AGENDA EACH DAY IS TO WALK WITH GOD.

States, he cannot fight his battle alone; he must discipline his life to remain close to God and distant from the world (James 4:8).

It is your duty as a pastor to be ever vigilant, taking heed to yourself and to the state of the flock. Caring for the spiritual needs of a congregation is a weighty responsibility, one for which you will give an account, as the writer of Hebrews made clear: *"Obey them that have the rule over you, and submit yourselves: for they watch for your soul, as they that must give account, that they may do it with joy, and not with grief: for that is unprofitable for you"* (Hebrews 13:17).

For pastors and missionaries, one facet of the battle is scrutinizing the media that influence us. We need to be familiar with the media-evangelists and the message they preach so that, when the occasion warrants, we can warn our people of deceptions that will turn their hearts and minds from the truth.

A PARTIAL TRUTH IS A WHOLE LIE.

Some nationally known authors and television pastors are offering an alleged Christianity that requires no repentance, no change—except maybe an inflated self-esteem—and, really, no hope for tomorrow.

We once had a member who listened regularly to a radio preacher who predicted the end of the earth and said the church was not for today. Needless to say, it was a painful experience to lose a good young couple to the false teaching of other preachers.

It is imperative that we make the Bible our absolute and final authority; therefore, let me share with you some absolute convictions one must lay down as the foundation of a biblical church. Whether you are the one starting a church or the established pastor supporting another pastor or missionary, these convictions must permeate and shape your very soul.

CONVICTION 1: THE CHURCH BELONGS TO JESUS CHRIST

The church of Jesus Christ has been described by the pen of the Apostle Paul as a body—a cohesive entity designed to bring glory to its head, Jesus Christ. As Paul reminded young Timothy, so I remind each of us, the church of the living God is the *"pillar and ground of the truth"* (1 Timothy 3:15). It is God's design. I remind us because it is so easy for a pastor to think of himself more highly than he ought to think and to regard the church as *his* church. If anything good ever comes of your ministry—and it will—you ought to thank Almighty God for it. It is not your ingenuity, your education, or your talents that cause the work to succeed. It is not you; it is God. He is the one who must get all the glory for anything and everything good that is accomplished.

That concept was easy for me because I had never accomplished anything before I was saved and went into the ministry. I wasn't a great student in school. I was on the bottom of the totem pole in the army. I never went into business. I never really succeeded at anything on my own—then God saved me and put me into the ministry! It was easy for me to be able to give God all the glory because I knew that I had never done anything worthwhile, and I am confident I never would have without the Lord. In a society afflicted with

> IT IS IMPERATIVE THAT WE MAKE THE BIBLE OUR ABSOLUTE AND FINAL AUTHORITY.

"me-itis," let us never steal any glory from the Lord and bestow it upon ourselves. He alone is worthy.

CONVICTION 2: PEOPLE WITHOUT CHRIST SPEND ETERNITY IN A CHRISTLESS HELL

Always keep in mind that the people who live where you are going to plant a church, as well as those all around the world, will spend their eternity in Hell if they are not saved. Church planters truly are on a search and rescue mission. We must have a sense of urgency in our hearts because there is no time to waste in this rescue operation. Keeping this in mind will help us when our bodies tell us to slow down and the devil tells us, "Take it easy. Don't be such a fanatic." Hell is real. The Bible says *"In flaming fire taking vengeance on them that know not God and that obey not the gospel of our Lord Jesus Christ"* (2 Thessalonians 1:8). People will die and go to Hell without the message of the Gospel that God has entrusted to us. We must be faithful (1 Corinthians 4:1–2).

May I remind all of us that this conviction must burden our hearts from day one and press on us until the Lord returns! It is so easy to slow down or back off as the church progresses along. If you find yourself bogged down with the many administrative duties required of a pastor, it is time to reassess your priorities. You must make time for souls and never let the devil douse the flame that burns to reach the lost at any cost. All ministers and servants must stay motivated and driven regarding this conviction.

CONVICTION 3: CHRIST ALONE CAN BUILD HIS CHURCH

The church has its origin in Matthew 16:18 where Jesus proclaimed, *"And I say also unto thee, That thou art Peter, and upon this rock I will build my church; and the gates of hell shall not prevail against it."* God doesn't need your help. He builds His church. He chooses to work through us to some degree, but the work is His doing. Never let a desire for man's approval put you into competition with God. You are not out there building something; God is doing the building. If you try to do it, failure is the forecast.

We all want more in attendance. We all want more than what we have, but we must learn that satisfaction and peace come from being in the perfect will of God. You can learn this lesson from admonition, or you can learn it the hard way— from firsthand experience.

I shall never forget preparing for our church's tenth year anniversary. We had everyone possible praying and fasting for our goal of 1,000 people in attendance. Our members worked so hard. Many spent long hours knocking on doors and inviting others. Sure enough, we had a great day on our bus routes and in our Sunday school classes. Our auditorium was packed to capacity and then some. It was an exciting morning!

We had prepared dinner so that everyone could join us right after the service. While I was eating, still musing over all the people in attendance, one of our men came to me and gleefully asked, "Pastor, do you want to know how many we had?" Of course, I could hardly wait to hear of the greatest attendance in our church history. He said, "We had 968!"

I responded with a less enthusiastic, "Thanks for telling me." I was so discouraged because I hadn't prayed for 968; I had prayed for 1,000! The Lord had more than doubled our attendance and allowed us to see many salvation decisions, but I felt let down. It took a couple of hours, but by the time the Holy Spirit finished with me, I was so ashamed for my lack of gratitude. I learned that I am to do all I can in faithfully serving God and then leave the results to Him. He is building *His* church, not mine. I am *His* servant; He is not mine. I am a vessel—that's all.

I have attended countless preachers' meetings in my years of ministering, and to this day, I have never had anyone ever ask me if I had the power of God upon me or if God's Spirit was at work in the services last week. I have, however, had many ask what our attendance was or how our offerings were. Many have asked about our building programs and various ministries, but not about that which is so vitally important for me as a preacher—God's power and Spirit at work in and through my life.

> I AM TO DO ALL I CAN IN FAITHFULLY SERVING GOD AND THEN LEAVE THE RESULTS TO HIM.

If I am working to boast of large attendances or healthy offerings, I am doing a fleshly work that won't please God. If I am to do God's work, I will accomplish it *only* by His power. Though you may be extremely talented, never try to build God's church on your ability. Mark it down, the work of the flesh will eventually falter.

I think all God-fearing men want to be found faithful at the end: *"…steadfast, unmoveable, always abounding in the work of the Lord…"* (1 Corinthians 15:58). This is why it is so important that we don't get sidetracked into thinking that we can do things our way, rather than His. Everyone needs the conviction that God builds His church, and if a man wants to be part of it, he will have to adopt His doctrine, His program, His methods, and His timing.

The verse that my son and I have claimed as our ministry verse to help us keep our values and priorities in place is 1 Corinthians 2:4: *"And my speech and my preaching was not with enticing words of man's wisdom, but in demonstration of the Spirit and of power."* This is what we want to be able to say about our ministries when we lay down our swords to be with Him. This verse serves as a constant reminder that the church is the Lord's work, not ours.

CONVICTION 4: I MUST LABOR WITH THE NUMBER ONE DESIRE OF PLEASING HIM

Pleasing our Lord should be goal number one. Yes, when I set out to plant Fairfax Baptist Temple, I wanted to please my sending church. I wanted to please my wife and family. I wanted to please my supporting churches, but more than anyone else, I wanted to please God. I knew that to do this I would have to demonstrate much faith, both in the birth of the church and its continuance.

Hebrews 11:6, expressing God's mind, reminds us that *"without faith it is impossible to please Him; for he that cometh to God must believe that He is, and that He is a rewarder of them that diligently seek Him."* I admonish you to keep your ministry a work of faith that will please God.

This matter of pleasing the Lord comes at the exclusion of trying to please any others, including you. At the outset, Satan will tempt you to seek the approval of man as opposed to the approval of God. This temptation can be very subtle. Many times accomplishing one's own agenda or goals can take precedence over accomplishing God's. Be extremely careful. Your success is determined by your obedience to God's wisdom, not to man's wishes; to the job He has called you to do, not to your own desires.

Please allow me to give a little five-point matrix for considering God's will in your ministry. The following are important Bible-based beliefs for each of us to espouse with the understanding that, ultimately and primarily, it is God we seek to please:

1. **Our Manual.** There has been and will continue to be debate over manuscript evidence and, therefore, the translation that is the best. As you can probably tell by the writing of this book, I use the King James Version of the Bible exclusively, believing the Byzantine family of manuscripts to be the best. Therefore, for preachers like me to use another version would be the epitome of trying to please others rather than the Lord. Generally, when one departs on this road, he will follow other detours as well.

Missionary-evangelist, you must find the best translation that you can in the people's language. I have heard testimony from so many men over the years about how greatly the ministry is hindered when only poor quality translations of the Bible are available. It is a delicate matter to correct errors without shaking the people's confidence in the written Word of God. Great discernment is necessary to protect against and correct erosion of essential doctrines while leaving alone errors that do not limit the sovereignty of God or the purity of the Gospel of Christ concerning salvation.

2. Our Music. As a pastor, you will have to decide the audience to whom the church is singing, whether it be God or man. Clearly, man prefers the music of the heathen culture from which we have all come—rock, country, hip-hop, etc.—to psalms, hymns, and spiritual songs. But our church music must reflect our faith in a holy God so that, in turn, we please Him in our worship with music.

3. Our Modesty. This is a matter of deciding on the standards you will require for leadership in the church. Some have the basic notion that having any kind of standards is "legalistic." I have noticed that when people use the word *legalist* to refer to another church or preacher, they are simply saying, "Your standards are higher than mine!" We all set standards. The question is this: from where do your standards come? As a pastor, young or old, you should get your modesty standards right from the Bible. If they aren't there, be careful about imposing them on others.

The other day, I called a golf course close to my home to ask if I could wear denim shorts. The attendant responded, "no." Their standard at the course is slacks and a collared shirt. I could have said, "Well, if those legalists won't let me wear denim and a t-shirt, I'll go elsewhere." As all golfers know, there is no "elsewhere"! I wanted to golf, so I accepted their standards and dressed accordingly.

We should train our people to accept the standards laid out in the Word of God as reasonable, just as they accept the dress standards set down at their job or the businesses they patronize.

4. Our Methods. Here is where many have departed from biblical thinking. Today rather than building churches on powerful, uncompromising preaching and leadership, many are relying on their charisma, programs, contemporary music, and basically anything else people want. God's Word still admonishes, "*Let every man take heed **how** he buildeth thereupon*" (1 Corinthians 3:10) (emphasis added). Methods do count!

The most often quoted line I hear from those who march to a different drumbeat is, "We may have changed our methods, but we'll never change our doctrine."

I would beg to differ. Many methods are based on doctrine. Consider for example the doctrine underlying the method of worship Cain and Abel were to follow. One method, which depicted Christ's sacrifice, was acceptable, and the other, which depicted man's works, was rejected. Remember the Bible story of Nadab and Abihu? They decided to rebel against the commandment of the Lord and worship in a new way, offering incense with fire not taken from the altar. Their only sin was doing a right thing in a wrong way. Their method was unacceptable to God, who clearly displayed His wrath at their rebellion by devouring them with fire. When Uzzah was struck dead for putting his hand out to steady the Ark of God, the men transporting the Ark also found out a little too late that God's method would have been the preferred way. And then there was Naaman the leper who was completely distraught by the method Elisha suggested to cure his leprosy. It was only after his servants talked him into accepting God's method that he was finally healed.

> THE GREATEST DOCTRINE IMPACTED BY OUR METHODS IS THE HOLINESS OF GOD.

The greatest doctrine impacted by our methods is the holiness of God. A good question to ask yourself is this: Do my methods exalt or diminish God's holiness?

5. Our Mission. World evangelism is another area in which we have the responsibility of pleasing God. It seems that even the Great Commission is being redefined by many. Rather than demonstrating a passion and burden to take the Gospel to a lost and dying world by sending out church planters, churches are diverting much of God's money to do a myriad of other things under the label of "missions." If we are going to please God in our worldwide outreach, then we are going to have to get back to the book of Acts and start planting more churches.

CONVICTION 5: EVERY HUMAN BEING IS WORTH HELPING AND HEALING, LOVING AND LEADING

If you don't have this conviction, you are not fit for the ministry. Learn to love the people that God gives you. Don't ever communicate to your congregation that you are so interested in reaching more people that you are not concerned about the ones you have. Don't let people think that you are so busy with world evangelism that you don't care about them. The men, ladies, and children; the married and single; the young and old; the sickly and strong are your church family. Remember you are the shepherd of a flock. It is important to love your people. Love can be spelled t-i-m-e. I highly recommend that you regularly visit your own people and invite them to your home. Get to know them by spending time with them.

The Lord's instruction to his disciples still applies to all of us today: "...*Go out quickly into the streets and lanes of the city, and bring in hither the poor, and the maimed, and the halt, and the blind*" (Luke 14:21). James expands that idea when he says that we are not to show "...*respect of persons*" (James 2:1). He continues:

> *For if there come unto your assembly a man with a gold ring, in goodly apparel, and there come in also a poor man in vile raiment; And ye have respect to him that weareth the gay clothing, and say unto him, Sit thou here in a good place; and say to the poor, Stand thou there, or sit here under my footstool; Are ye not*

then partial in yourselves, and are become judges of evil thoughts? —JAMES 2:2–4

Yes, we are to go after the poor and the suffering; however, we must not forget the rich man! We are not to play up to them, but we are not to neglect them either.

Some of my best memories are those of when I was a college student, working a bus route in a mill area where most of the people were quite poor. A few children lived on the outskirts of our route, and Mary, Troy, and I would go pick them up in our car to take them to a location on the bus route. After church before returning home, the first thing I had to do was spray air-freshener directly into the fabric of my car because of the odor that was left. But those were great days because many of those precious souls received Christ as their Saviour.

When God sent me to Fairfax in Northern Virginia, I soon found out that there were no poor people. Our county had, and still has, the highest income per family of any county in the United States. Instead of "down-and-outers," we had "up-and-outers!" Everyone should be treated with genuine love and dignity. God loves them all and so should we.

Remember your ministry is one of people. Accept them where you find them, and lead them to where they need to be. That is what a pastor and a missionary does. The church is always in a state of flux. We have some who just got saved and others who have been saved fifty years. Some are happy families, and others are dysfunctional. We don't all get to the same maturity level at the same time. Love all people right where they are, with their problems, struggles, and difficulties.

CONVICTION 6: I MUST BE A FAITHFUL MAN OF GOD, REGARDLESS

"Therefore, my beloved brethren, be ye stedfast, unmoveable, always abounding in the work of the Lord forasmuch as ye know that your labour is not in vain in the Lord" (1 Corinthians 15:58). *"Moreover it is required in stewards, that a man be found faithful"* (1 Corinthians 4:2). Don't get sidetracked in your ministry. Stay faithful to God, your family, and your church. It really is important that you don't step out on your own and forget your wife and children. You should work together and serve God together in the ministry.

Having retired from pastoring full-time, I can tell you that being a pastor or missionary-evangelist is difficult and demanding work if done competently. To the lay people: Do you remember the stress of having to prepare and deliver speeches in school? A pastor has the responsibility of preparing and preaching a new message for every Sunday morning, Sunday evening, and Wednesday night service. Most also have to prepare and teach a Sunday school lesson. In our ministry, I also taught once or twice a week in our Bible college and then did a fifteen-minute live radio broadcast five days a week, besides speaking at weddings, funerals, chapel, and other occasions. My point is that to spend the necessary time for message preparation, counseling, visitation, staff meetings, deacon meetings, and administration of the church, one needs to be extremely time-conscious and plan each day well.

Typically my schedule operated like this: Monday was my day off; Tuesdays and Thursdays (or other necessary times) were spent on administration, counseling, and hospital visits; Wednesdays were dedicated to staff meetings and preparation for Wednesday night. Friday I usually spent all day preparing Sunday night's message; and Saturday I spent all day preparing Sunday morning's message and Sunday school lesson. I went visiting on Tuesday and Thursday evenings and also on Saturday, depending on how I was doing with my preparation for Sunday.

Ask God for wisdom as you list and schedule your priorities so that you can accomplish everything He wants you to do to His honor and glory.

If you make these six points your own convictions, God promises you a fruitful and successful ministry. In Acts 20:24 the Bible says, *"But none of these things move me, neither count I my life dear unto myself, so that I might finish my course with joy, and the ministry, which I have received of the Lord Jesus, to testify the gospel of the grace of God."* Paul's self-abandonment enabled him to say these words, and I pray that each one of us will be able to speak these words as well.

> ONE NEEDS TO BE EXTREMELY TIME-CONSCIOUS AND PLAN EACH DAY WELL.

BUDGETING

*For which of you, intending to build
a tower, sitteth not down first, and
counteth the cost, whether he have
sufficient to finish it?*
—LUKE 14:28

To illustrate the need to weigh out the sacrifices of discipleship, Jesus uses the example of building a tower as a metaphor. He says that before starting a construction project, a man should do two things. First, he should sit down. Second, he should count the cost. In other words, he should plan. Planning involves looking ahead and making choices. This is essential for the sending church, the new church yet to be planted, and it is also essential for the new church planter's personal finances.

Think about the requirements for a bishop set out in 1 Timothy 3:4. Someone seeking to be a bishop must be *"One that ruleth well his own house, having his children in subjection with all gravity."* We always look at the second half of the verse but largely ignore the first phrase. Part of ruling a household is

129

having control over the family finances. If you cannot manage your family on a budget, how do you expect to manage the church's finances according to a budget? The old adage is true: "Failing to plan is planning to fail."

This chapter consists of three parts. I start with the church planter's personal finances because it is the only area I, as a sending pastor, can examine to see if the candidate has the personal maturity and self-control to be a trustworthy steward of God's household of faith. Supporting churches should not be expected to pay for things purchased in the past, and discretionary debt is an indication that the man has not yet learned to wait on God to provide his every need. For these reasons, we will not send out a man who has discretionary debt. If a man can't keep his own personal finances in order, how will he be able to oversee the church's finances?

PERSONAL BUDGET FOR CHURCH PLANTERS

As a young pastor, you should not strive for wealth as we define that term in an earthly or material sense. The goal you should strive for is that you and your family live in contentment. Paul gave this counsel to his son in the faith:

> But godliness with contentment is great gain. For we
> brought nothing into this world, and it is certain we
> can carry nothing out. And having food and raiment
> let us be therewith content. But they that will be rich
> fall into temptation and a snare, and into many foolish

and hurtful lusts, which drown men in destruction and perdition. For the love of money is the root of all evil: which while some coveted after, they have erred from the faith, and pierced themselves through with many sorrows. But thou, O man of God, flee these things; and follow after righteousness, godliness, faith, love, patience, meekness.—1 TIMOTHY 6:6–11

One of my favorite quotes of all time is by C.S. Lewis in his sermon entitled "The Weight of Glory." He said, "...it must be true, as an old writer says, that he who has God and everything else has no more than he who has God only." When you have God, you have it all! If you have anything in addition, it is really superfluous for ministry and personal growth. This truth is a great one to keep in mind anytime you're dealing with finances. God is your provider and sustainer.

> THE GOAL YOU SHOULD STRIVE FOR IS THAT YOU AND YOUR FAMILY LIVE IN CONTENTMENT.

Don't let anything distract you from God's goodness to you. Things, material wealth, are just that—a distraction.

Early in our ministry, one of the men in our church offered to build Mary and me a house at his cost. We were thrilled, and after we found a piece of land to build on, the house was under way. The gentleman building the house for us was sincere and very thoughtful even to offer us such a favor. However, a month after we moved into this beautiful home, he told me that there had been a mistake due to a change of bookkeepers and that the actual cost for our house was about 30 percent more than had been expected.

My wife had just finished sewing the last drapery when I came home to tell her the news. Her response echoed my first thought, "Let's just sell it then." We could have made the payments, but it would have strapped us so much that we would not have had the extra funds that we enjoy giving to the Lord and others. So six weeks after we moved into our custom built home, it was on the market for sale! God honored that decision with an even better home later, and the experience helped us to inventory our priorities and values in life.

When it comes to finances, our theme should be *"godliness with contentment."* Keep that in mind if you consider buying a house when you are just planting a new church that isn't yet able to provide full salary, housing allowance, health benefits, retirement, and so forth. Even if you don't buy a house, be careful about renting a more expensive apartment than you need for the first year or so. Prudence is required to avoid becoming so financially committed that you do not have the flexibility to do other things, personal or ministry-related. *"Let your conversation* [manner or deportment] *be without covetousness: and be content with such things as ye have..."* (Hebrews 13:5).

Financial planning is nothing more than allocating your limited resources to accomplish your predetermined goals. Normally, people who get into financial difficulties are those who do not budget or do not discipline themselves to stick to a budget. The younger you are the more important it is to keep your life on track with a budget. Sticking with a budget will help you get through the first twenty or so years of adult life, to a stage when finances are not so tight. Most people don't have enough money when they are young and have children to care for, but do when they are older and don't need it as much. That's when old people start spending their children's inheritance on whatever they want!

> FINANCIAL PLANNING IS NOTHING MORE THAN ALLOCATING YOUR LIMITED RESOURCES TO ACCOMPLISH YOUR PREDETERMINED GOALS.

You and your wife need to work as a team in all areas of your marriage, but especially in the area of financial management. One of the things a man needs most in marriage is the respect of his wife, and one of the things a woman needs most is the love and security she gets from her husband. There is probably only one thing that shakes a woman's feelings of security more than financial worries (marital infidelity). You can work to remove these worries by involving her in the family financial decisions. Your wife, assuming she is 100 percent supportive of the church planting endeavor (and, as I said earlier, if she is not, then don't even think about trying to be a church planter), will be willing to sacrifice along with you in the early days if she understands that you have a plan that puts your family's well-being at the top of the list. I am not talking about extravagance. I still echo Paul's admonition for contentment, but a large part of contentment is knowing that you have a plan. Your budget is that plan. Together, you need to set it in place and then work it. There is a sample personal budget template at the end of this chapter that you can use for planning your financial needs.

When starting a church, you need to be thinking about survival—how much it will take to stay alive. That's all you should concern yourself with. After the church is planted, you might be able to eat two meals a day! Your initial budget should be a bare-bones budget that demonstrates that you and your wife are willing to sacrifice for the Lord's work. If the Lord supplies beyond that, then praise Him for it!

Develop good habits so that they become second nature to you. Avoid buying things on impulse. My advice to all church planters is not to be too proud to shop in secondhand stores and not to become enamored with name brands. It's amazing how much people spend on name brand clothing, even when they haven't sufficiently saved for emergencies, college, reserves, or retirement. Now after forty years of ministry, I still can't keep my wife out of Goodwill and Salvation Army stores. They were a necessity for a long time, but now they are simply a choice she can't do without!

Also avoid using credit cards if you find that you are unable to pay the bill in full each month. A good practice is to write the amount charged in your checkbook or ledger as if you had already paid for your purchase. For that matter, if you want to use a card, use a debit card instead of a credit card. That way, you take advantage of some of the purchase protection of credit cards, but you do not spend money that you do not have. I know it sounds unpatriotic, but my wife and I did not even own a credit card the first fifteen years we were married. Then, to show we were real Americans, we got one. We have used it for thirty years, but we've never paid one cent of interest on it because we pay it off each month!

Your personal budget should reflect faith, reality, humility, and contentment. You should work out this one-year budget with the sending church. The income side is based on income from your sending church, other churches, other sources like relatives who want to help, an outside job if necessary, personal savings and assets, and possibly, potential income from the new church.

Because none of us has the same background as another, you should not try to compare your situation with someone else's. If you are older when God calls you to start a church, you probably have some equity in your house that will help immensely in purchasing another house. If you have a large sending church behind you, then more than likely, you will have a good (livable) income immediately. It may be that your wife will be able to work outside the home to help with the family income. (Do not consider this option if there are children who would have to go to a sitter or who are young enough to require your time at home taking care of them. Rather than taking them to some kind of a day care, finding work you can do at home might be a better solution.) Perhaps you have rich relatives who want to help (quit dreaming!). Simply put, no two scenarios are exactly the same.

When I started, I worked out what the late Bro. Grant Rice called a "Survival Budget," that is, a bare-bones approach to our financial needs. Mary and I figured out that we could live on $85 a week (back in 1970). At the time, I didn't know that other churches would often help new churches getting started. I was praying all along that somehow the Lord would provide this amount. One church promised support of $50 a month, and a Sunday school class promised $25 a month support. As it turned out, the church stopped sending support after three months, and we are still waiting for the Sunday school class to send us their first $25!

It is so wonderful today that there is an emphasis on church planting in the United States as well as overseas. It makes it much easier (notice I said easier, not easy) to present your burden and raise support. If you go around to other churches to raise support, be careful never to solicit or accept monthly support from individuals. If people want to support you, ask them to do it through their church with their pastor's full knowledge and support.

You should start weaning yourself from outside support as soon as possible. Encourage your young church to start taking you on for support as soon as they are able. The new church may give you the best benefit by providing health insurance, car allowance, etc. instead of salary, as those other benefits may be free of tax to you. It doesn't take much. If you have just two or three tithing families, you can start drawing a salary or have the church provide support benefits. We have sent out church planters who were able to be fully supported by their new church in as little as one month, five months, or a year, though most take longer. Some have taken over ten years to be fully supported by their new church. Some have received support from our church the full three years, but of course, our overseas church planters receive ongoing monthly support because they continue to need it as they plant more churches.

The summer before starting the church, I came across the Bible verse that says, *"Even so hath the Lord ordained that they which preach the gospel should live of the gospel"* (1 Corinthians 9:14). I determined then, by faith, that when it was time to start the church, I was going to be supported full-time by the church. Mary and I sold the trailer we lived in while in college before we made our move to Fairfax, Virginia. After paying for living expenses, apartment rent, and escrow, we had a little left over. So the first Sunday we started our church, I put $100 in the offering plate just to make sure I received a pay check and could say I was in the ministry as a full-time pastor! The Lord blessed that first week and every week thereafter.

SENDING CHURCH BUDGET

A part of the responsibility of a church that is sending out a church planter is to help him on his way—to invest in the new church by supporting the new pastor financially. There should be a spirit of ready cooperation by the pastor and sending church to help a young man setting out on this adventure of a lifetime. Paul was sent out of the church at Antioch. The Scriptures do not give an account of that church's financial support for Paul's church planting efforts. Paul, however, does commend one church for its support:

> *Now ye Philippians know also, that in the beginning of the gospel, when I departed from Macedonia, no church communicated with me as concerning giving and receiving, but ye only. For even in Thessalonica ye*

sent once and again unto my necessity. Not because I
desire a gift: but I desire fruit that may abound to your
account.—PHILIPPIANS 4:15–17

One principle of biblical finance is this: whatever God asks us to accomplish, He also finances. A problem arises when established churches do not consider the fact that they are a key link in helping young men fulfill God's calling to start a church on the mission field or here in America. It is a matter of priorities, and what is important to us will be reflected in the budgets of our churches, the sending churches and other supporting churches as well.

It is an expensive proposition for a sending church to get behind a church planter. Though it is costly, it is perhaps the greatest investment a church can make. Certainly it will make a difference for the church planter and his family and also for the area in which they will be ministering. The church at Philippi made a difference when they sent to Paul's necessity "once and again." Each church will have to decide what it can do with its limited resources. The only thing God expects is our best.

God has wonderfully blessed the ministry of the Fairfax Baptist Temple beyond anything that I could have ever asked or dreamed. In everything—people, finances, and facilities—we have been abundantly blessed. So I am writing from my perspective when I say that a sending church should do as much as it can about taking on the new church planter's salary. I don't want to be unfair to other churches and suggest that they don't love the Lord as much as we do, because that is not true. I am simply saying that God expects us to make church planting priority number one in our endeavors to evangelize the world.

The sending church should be ready to sacrifice because supporting a church planter is a heavy financial investment, but keep in mind that this is an eternal investment—one that will continue to reap dividends. The sending pastor must fully involve his heart in this ministry for it to succeed. Without his backing, the "plane will never get off

THE ONLY THING GOD EXPECTS IS OUR BEST.

the runway." It is important for the pastor to lead his church into participation and commitment. I mentioned earlier that church planting is a partnership, a "we" proposition. No one should be in it alone. With this understanding, there should be a willingness to be flexible even in financial matters. Most churches will be limited in what they can do, but all churches can probably do more than they are presently doing. No question about it, we are living in precarious days, spiritually, economically, politically, and morally. Our present condition is all the more reason to expect the soon return of our resurrected Saviour and to invest all we can in His work before He appears!

Sacrifice is often painful, but we are to be reminded again that everything we have comes from the Lord. *"The earth is the Lord's and the fullness thereof; the world, and they that dwell therein"* (Psalm 24:1). None of us should cling tightly to what the Lord has given us, but with open hands and open hearts, everyone should bow before the Lord to discern his part.

One area in which a church may sacrifice is sending its own people to help a starting church. At the Fairfax Baptist Temple we actually encourage our church planters to try to recruit some families to go with them, under pastoral direction. I know how much it meant to me to have Dave and Margaret Abbey at our first meeting when we had a total of six people: my wife and son and Dave and his wife and son! As it turned out, they assisted Mary and me in almost everything. So we tell everyone who is going out to start a church to start praying for someone to go with them.

When families leave the sending church to go help the new church planter, it is a wonderful thing for both churches. I have to admit that it took me a while before I felt that way. Our church has always been a family and to see a family member go to another church, even one of our own, was always a little painful. However, I am sure what the new pastor and church gains is far greater than what the sending church loses. We have had many families go with our church planters through the years, and what we have found is that often the ones who go with the new pastor really come alive with enthusiasm and a servant's heart to help.

We sent out a church planter to a part of our community that was just over twenty miles away. While this is not the normal situation, he went there at my encouragement because I knew the area needed another good church and also because I knew we had a good number of families living out that way. When the new church started, there were about a dozen of our families that went with him. Needless to say, losing that many families impacted not only our numbers and our finances but also our work force because many of them were faithful workers in the ministry as well. Some other families joined with him right away creating a ready-made church. I say this to point out that the needs of new churches differ. We needed to support that new pastor for only two months before the church he planted was able to support him. It had never happened quite that way before.

A man we sent out to another state received eight families from a pastor and church because our pastor had located nearer to where these families lived. We were so grateful for the big heart of this pastor to help in the beginning of this church as well. After five or six months, the new pastor called and said he didn't need support any longer. Amen! Others have been supported by their new church after the first year, but most take much longer. Some, even after three years of support, are not able to receive full-time support from their churches. Usually these take on a part-time job to help supplement their income.

Some of the following items may be a part of the sending church's budget for the support of the new pastor. What I am not discussing here is the investment that has already been made in training the new pastor as an intern. This is strictly looking at helping the new pastor "get out the door." No new pastor should assume the sending church has the responsibility for all of these things.

BUDGET CONSIDERATIONS AND COMMENTARY

PRINTING

Following this section is a list of items to print. While your initial inkling might be to print as many as possible of each item, you must consider one important factor before determining the number you need: How permanent is your temporary meeting place? Most of our men have moved from their first meeting place within a year. Therefore, if you think the motel or school you are renting may not offer longevity, you might want to consider printing fewer materials at first so that you don't have to paste over the old address or location. If you are definitely temporary in your first building, you might use a P.O. Box to receive mail. But so people can find your location, you will have to include a separate map and address of your physical location with your materials. Make sure the telephone number you print is permanent. Many of our men are now using their cell phone with a local number.

For your first printing, I suggest about 25,000 each of the following (except stationery) to be passed out on your Gospel Blitz and an additional 5,000 to use as you go door-to-door later. After you are in a more permanent place you may want to print some additional material. Keep in mind that we are now living in an "information" society in which people are more apt to read. Therefore, do not settle for anything less than high quality material with the finest graphics, color, and paper. You will want to have the following on hand:

- Tracts
- Flyers
- Brochures
- Gospel of John and Romans
- Stationery

ADVERTISING

You only get one chance to make a good first impression. With that in mind, you should operate with the philosophy that quality is better than quantity. Use professionals to design your advertising. Don't fool yourself into thinking, "No one would ever guess that I did it myself," because they will! Realizing you have a limited budget, seek advice about how to use your advertising money. Spend your advertising dollars carefully.

Certainly having a great web page is important today (in all first-world countries and many third-world countries). If you are meeting in a large facility, you will definitely need signs to direct people at the entrance of the facility and in the hallways. Weigh out the value of each of the following, placing them in order of importance to you:

- Mail-outs
- Newspaper ads
- Radio ads
- Television ads
- Phone book ads
- Web page
- Signs

EQUIPMENT

Most new churches in the United States or overseas will need all or many of the following items. You may, with the permission of the pastor, present the need for these things to different churches. More than likely, you will find churches that would be glad to purchase these items for you. Give each item a price tag when you present it. Perhaps someone may have a piano or keyboard that they would like to contribute so that you won't have to spend money on one. Concerning donated items, my advice is to use only those in nearly perfect condition. I have seen churches contribute old hymnals or battered offering plates that I would not use. You don't want first-time visitors to walk in and find on their chair an old, tattered hymnal that has the name of another church on it! If you receive such donations, respond politely and get some new ones. The same goes for chairs and the other items listed below.

- Podium
- Hymnals
- Offering plates
- Cribs
- Piano/keyboard
- Chairs

RENTAL DEPOSIT

This is usually your first month's building rent and perhaps a deposit they would hold in an escrow account just to make sure they can cover the cost if something is damaged. You also want to make sure you have sufficient liability insurance for the place in which you are meeting.

TRAVEL EXPENSES FOR THE PASTOR AND STAFF WHO PARTICIPATE

Some churches that have started out of our church have been close enough that we could drive to it and take our ministerial staff. In most cases, there will be expenses for transportation and motels.

SET-UP COSTS AND OTHER INCIDENTALS

If the sending church has the resources, they may wish to help with some of the incidental expenses that go with the start-up costs of a new church—including moving and living expenses for the pastor and family (who will probably move about a month before starting), new phones, commentaries, post office mail-box, and office needs (e.g., computer, printer etc.). One thing we always do the night of the new pastor's commissioning is receive an offering of several thousand dollars and give it to him for these very things.

NEW PASTOR'S SALARY

What we normally do is continue the salary we have been paying them as interns. This provides continuity for the family going out and cuts down on the time, if any, they have to spend on deputation. Your church may not be in a position to do this, but you should try to do as much as possible to reduce the time they will have to spend seeking support.

You may wish to make a financial commitment for the first twelve months, at which time everything would be reviewed. At Fairfax Baptist Temple, we talk to the pastor after twelve months to find out (if we don't already know) exactly where he stands with support. We take into consideration how much outside money he has coming in and how much his new church is able to support him. Proportional to his needs, we try to cut back the amount we are supporting him to encourage his church to get serious about their responsibility to take care of him.

The new pastor should start to reduce his support earlier if the new church is able to pick up more of his salary. It is great for the new pastor when his church senses the responsibility to provide for him.

NEW CHURCH BUDGET

Let's face it, gentlemen, most of us have had little or no formal training on the subject of finances. There are some good books out on the subject now, and you would do yourself a great service by mastering it. Although you may not be involved in the minutia of your church's budget later on, you need to understand some basic budgetary principles so that you can lead in this area.

As I mentioned earlier, my belief has always been, "He who controls the finances, controls the church." When I talk about the one who controls the finances, I mean the one who has veto power over the budget, not the one who walks around saying, "I am in charge!" If you have to say that, your very statement proves that you are *not* in charge! It is also important that you never develop the attitude that says, "I don't need to be accountable to anyone." That is simply a formula for disaster. One can never be too careful in the area of finances.

Every new church needs to have a budget. It gives accountability and responsibility. One reason having a budget is important to the new church is that people considering the new church are more likely to review the budget than those considering an established church. When we first started, people often asked to see the budget, but I cannot recall how long it has been since anyone joining Fairfax Baptist Temple asked to see the budget first. Once the church is established, when it has members and buildings, people assume that it is financially stable.

Maybe you are like me—just thinking about sitting down to plan a budget is something I do not enjoy. Whichever spiritual gift that falls under, I don't have it! I found it helpful in the early days to consider the process an opportunity to inspire the membership. Your budget, in addition to being the plan for funding the present operation of the church, is a means to impart your vision for the future. The first budget is very important because it communicates the heart of the new church, which, at this point, is the heart of the pastor.

The budget will communicate ministry opportunities as well. As a church grows, so do opportunities to minister for our Lord. Almost every year, ministries that need funding will be added, and by showing them on the budgetary guidelines, you will be presenting more opportunities. For instance, about a year after our church started, we launched a bus ministry. When we put money for that ministry in our budget, we introduced opportunities for being a bus captain, helper, driver, or mechanic. There may be a new line on your budget for children's church. While you are going over the expenses (for materials, chairs, snacks, etc.), you

> THE FIRST BUDGET IS IMPORTANT BECAUSE IT COMMUNICATES THE HEART OF THE NEW CHURCH.

can mention the need for workers to help. The same is true for every other ministry you start or expand. Pastor, when you go over the budget, don't just talk about numbers, but emphasize the importance of the ministry and the opportunities they will afford more members to serve.

Communicating to the new church about finances is of utmost importance. When you discuss finances with the church, you might consider calling your budget "Financial Guidelines," as we do. It sounds a little less rigid and allows flexibility, which is especially needed in a new church. The pastor can mention several aspects of the budget when he receives the offering each week for the first few months. Doing so helps the people to see that there are real needs.

> AN INFORMED PEOPLE ARE A CONTENTED PEOPLE.

Actually, when we started our church, I discussed the budget in the Sunday school class the first Sunday. You don't have to do it that early, but I recommend that you cover it in the first month. In so doing, you will provide complete financial disclosure, as well as cast a vision of what you see for the church in the not too distant future.

Keeping people abreast of the financial progress encourages those who are giving and encourages those who have not started giving to do so. Put the total of all monies received in the next week's bulletin. Also, make copies of the budget available to all who are interested. An informed people are a contented people. The very moment your church thinks that you're trying to hide something, they will quit giving. Talk about your finances. Financial disclosure is a must!

A *clearly defined* budget is also a must for any church because people want to know what their money is going to when they give. Although most people would rather give toward "felt" needs, such as new hymnals, carpet, or a piano, it is important to let people know that when they tithe, they are not giving to a church or pastor; rather, they are giving to God through the church. They need to learn scriptural mandates about giving and the joy that comes with obeying God. I read an article about tithing, which asserted that the average churchgoer believes the church won't miss his money if he doesn't tithe. It is not a matter of whether the church will miss his money, but a matter of obedience to God's Word. Go ahead and present specific "felt" needs to encourage people to give *beyond* their tithe.

Putting together a clearly defined budget is not an easy task since you have no assurance of what your first few weeks will be like or how many, if any, will attend. Your budget items will represent good faith goals to strive for and should reflect both faith and reality. The initial budget should be designed to last until you have a good understanding of how many people are coming and how much money is coming in. Later in the chapter, I give a breakdown of the church budget to help you with your planning. You may have a better idea of your financial standing after only a few months. Then you should have a budget-planning meeting with the men who have become members of your church.

About ten weeks after starting our church, I met with all the men who were members to discuss updating our budget.

The initial budget I had planned got us through the first few months, but now it was time to involve more people. I actually explained what each line item was and how it fit into the scope of things. Now that we had a better handle on what was coming in each week, we were in a better position to launch forward in our endeavors.

One of the things we needed to deal with was my own personal support. I found presenting my personal needs to be very awkward. I have found that it is extremely uncomfortable for most of us to talk about what the church can do for us. We don't want to appear unspiritual or worldly because, after all, the Lord will provide! Well He does in every case, but the Bible also says that *"if any provide not for his own, and specially for those of his own house, he hath denied the faith, and is worse than an infidel"* (1 Timothy 5:8). In some denominations the pastor's salary and compensation package is already prescribed. But in others, as it is with independent Baptists, it is decided by each individual congregation. It is not that your church doesn't want to take care of you and your family needs, it is just that some people come into your church with the presupposition that someone else is taking care of the need, and therefore, it may be left undone. My point is don't hesitate to talk to your men/church about some of your current needs. They may simply be unaware of your struggles, and more than likely, they would love to help meet those needs.

From that very first meeting, the role you play in the church finances will change as the church grows. During the first five to ten years, I made a point of knowing everything about our budget. However, as the years passed and our church budget got larger, I relied very heavily on my Minister of Finance, who worked with me full time. He was the best in the country and gave me good advice. I would never go into a building program without his sound financial counsel. If you can't hire someone on staff later to help with the finances, don't hesitate to engage the services of a CPA or a volunteer bookkeeper.

Of course, you will need help handling the money from the very beginning. I would encourage you, as a pastor, to never actually handle any of the monies. I personally have never handled one nickel of the money received in our church. You must have the procedures set up *before* the first meeting and, if at all possible, reviewed with the persons—note that I said *persons*—who will be handling the money. You don't want to simply put the offering plates in the back, take them home, and put the money in the bank the next morning. No indeed. Money management is an issue you need to have fully predetermined.

From the very first day you start a church, have at least two people count the money—even in the evening—and sign a pre-printed sheet on which they put the date and offering totals. At the end of this chapter is a sheet that can be used by the men counting the money to make sure that every specially designated offering is properly documented. This sheet provides accountability. Never have just one person handling money received until it is placed in the secure bank deposit bag provided when you opened the account.

I can hear you asking, "Who do I get to count the money? Everyone is a stranger to me." I hope you were able to get a family or two to come with you to start the church. If you were able, the answer is obvious. If you were not then I suggest that you have a couple of men from your sending church count and sign the sheet.

On the first Sunday it is more than likely that you will have someone there who shows some real promise to become a regular attendee and member. Lord willing you may even have two! If so ask them if they could help in this important area and then put the offerings in the locked bank deposit bag. If you find only one person ask him to stay behind with you to count the money. Then both of you should sign the sheet. It shouldn't take long before God gives you a couple of good men to do this for you every service. I would also make sure in those early months that all offerings are left up front, somewhere visible by your pulpit, until after the service, and then have the two men count it together.

Another particular to consider is the church's checking account. It would be unwise for you, as the pastor, to sign checks. Some pastors feel it necessary to have double signatures with theirs being one of them. This is totally unnecessary and not recommended at all. If you don't get anything else, get this: the one thing you want to make sure of is that whoever does sign the checks is not the one who balances the checkbook. The two should never be done by the same person or department.

One final note regarding financial matters: I have made it a policy from the very beginning never to know how much any member contributes. My reasoning is that I don't ever want to give anyone the impression that I have been bought, and I don't ever want someone's giving to influence my decisions. I want nothing more than the full leading of God in my life. I'm sure that is your desire as well.

NEW CHURCH BUDGET BREAKDOWN

FACILITIES

- Rent/Lease: Of course this amount will depend on what kind of facilities you find. Be careful that you do not over commit yourself in this area. If you aren't sure, do with less.
- Utilities
- Office space to rent

ADMINISTRATION

All of these categories should include your estimate of how much will be needed on a weekly basis until the end of the year, at which time, you will make up and vote on a new Financial Guideline.

- Office Supplies
- Postage
- Bulletins
- Phone
- Computer and printer

ADVERTISING

- Yellow Pages ad
- Newspaper ad
- Web Page
- Gospel Blitz materials for continuing saturation of your community
- Tracts (This will go under another category later, but it can go here in the beginning.)

ANNUAL AUDIT (OR FINANCIAL REVIEW)

It is important to have your books audited by an outside auditing firm. If you want good credibility, this is a must. The truth of the matter is that a "review" is all that is needed yearly until you get ready to build. A review costs about half as much as an audit and is thorough enough for all practical purposes. In an audit, the firm calls some members to verify gifts and some venders to verify certain transactions, but these things are not necessary unless you are trying to get a bank loan. Most banks will require an audit to verify your assets, liabilities, and equity. This costs money, but in the long run it is well worth it.

For obvious reasons you don't want to get a church member or friend to audit your books. Hire a firm that is not associated with your church. It would be wise to go to an auditor at the very beginning of a church plant to ask for some advice on setting up your books. Then continue to seek counsel whenever you need it.

INSURANCE

- Liability insurance: This is an absolute must. It will cover you and the church for lawsuits resulting from someone sustaining an injury on your property. Because accidents can happen in the nurseries, classrooms, playgrounds, and other locations, it would be a good idea to check with an attorney so that you can know what to ask for in an insurance policy to make sure everything is covered. Of course, it is mandatory from the first day for whoever works with the nursery and children's ministry to have a police background and health check. The first person to have this done will probably be the pastor's wife, but just make sure it is done.

- Renter's insurance: Your coverage would depend on the kind of place you rent.

PASTOR

I suggest that the first budget include the following breakdown in order for everyone to understand the pastor's needs and requirements. As you add staff members, you will lump the salaries together. Of course, the men of the church, deacons and/or Compensation Committee (this is the only standing committee our church has) know exactly what your salary and the other staff salaries are, but I suggest you eliminate listing them separately for the privacy/protection of the staff. Everyone will have his opinion about what each person's compensation should be, based on his own, without really understanding the various offices. When you decide on staff salaries, there are two things that I think are important to consider: what is the staff member's value (significance, importance) to you as the pastor and what is his value to the overall ministry.

- Housing allowance: It has been my observation over the years that this matter is greatly misunderstood by many pastors. The IRS allows us, just as they do for the military, to disallow the amount of money we spend on housing from our income. Therefore, we do not have to pay taxes on that which we spend on housing. However, this is not a license to designate from your income the housing allowance you desire, to pay a huge mortgage payment or put hundreds (thousands) more on your mortgage to pay it off early. The statute reads that we are allowed no more than the "fair market rental value of the furnished home" plus the utilities. In other words, you can designate no more than what someone would pay to rent your home furnished. It is also required by law that you have a letter in writing that states x amount of money is designated to you as housing allowance. If your housing goes over that amount, you cannot deduct it. You are not allowed to exceed whatever you have in writing. If your housing is under the amount deducted on your 1040, and you do not use it all for housing, you must show it as "other income" and pay taxes on it. My comments are not meant to be legal advice but simply encouragement to do the right thing. Check with an attorney or CPA for more information.

- Car allowance: There are two things to consider here: owning a car and maintaining one. The simplest way to set up a car allowance, particularly in the beginning, may be to follow the government standard for reimbursement for business expenses. Whether the church purchases your car or you own it outright, you must keep accurate documentation, recording every mile used for business. If your church does purchase a vehicle for you, you must keep track of personal and business use. You will then need to get a 1099 from the church at the end of the year for the "personal" use of your car.

- Hospitalization: Make sure you and everyone on your staff have good hospitalization. The new church, at first, may not be able to put much down for this item, but listing it will help the church see that they need to be thinking about taking care of you and your family.
- Salary

CONFERENCE EXPENSE

- Conferences the pastor attends: Every pastor needs to attend at least one conference to be refreshed and challenged each year. Look for one that offers some "how to's" and encouragement. Include enough money to take your wife with you. Depending on your convictions about ecumenicalism, you should be careful about who is invited to the conference you are considering. I would want to fellowship with those of like faith, even if someone else seems to have a bigger and better program.
- Meetings with people: These conferences are often one-on-one lunches or dinners with people to meet all kinds of needs. I have met over lunch with a man when I am trying to reach him for the Lord. I have also used these meetings for the purpose of recruiting an individual or a couple for a particular ministry in the church. Sometimes the purpose of the meeting is counseling or encouragement, or it can simply be a great time of fellowship with different men in the church.

ACTIVITIES

In each of the following activities it would be wise to list some specifics such as "Couples Retreat," or "Teen Ski Trip" or "Children's Bicycle Hike."

- Adult activities
- Teen activities
- Children's activities

CHILDREN'S EDUCATION/CLUB PROGRAM

BUILDING PROGRAM

From the very beginning you should have a building category. This is vision casting and lets people know that you are a driven man with faith that the Lord is going to provide real estate and buildings. At first, you may only put in a few dollars a month, but you should definitely have it in your budget.

MISSIONS

You should consider keeping this category completely separate from the general fund to demonstrate that the offerings contributed are not being used for the general operation of the church. Also consider funding it with "grace giving" (often called "faith promise") from the very beginning. Grace giving encourages people to give above their tithes and offerings to help support worldwide evangelism. You may be the only one participating until you teach the others, usually at your first annual missions conference.

Personal Budget

	Jan 8	Jan 22	Feb 5	Feb 19
INCOME				
Outside Church Support				
New Church Support				
Other Income				
Cash on Hand				
TOTAL INCOME	0	0	0	0
EXPENSES				
Giving				
Tithes & Offerings				
Missions				
Building Fund				
Academy				
Housing				
Mortgage/Rent				
Condo/Homeowners Fee				
Electric				
Gas				
Water				
Trash				
Telephone				
Auto payments				
Insurance				
Taxes, Tags				
Gas/Bus $				
Loans/Credit Cards				
VISA/MC				
Bank				
Credit Union				
Educational				
Medical				
Doctor				
Dentist				
Tax-Self Emp				
Savings				
Others Fund				
Allowance				
Wife				
Husband				
TOTAL EXPENSE	0	0	0	0
Payday Net	0	0	0	0

OFFERING COUNTERS

Date: _____   ☐ SPANISH

Service: *Please check (✓) the appropriate box.*

☐ Sunday AM   ☐ Monday   ☐ Wednesday   ☐ Friday
☐ Sunday PM   ☐ Tuesday   ☐ Thursday   ☐ Saturday

TITHES & OFFERINGS

< _____ , ___ > 45000 Academy
< _____ , ___ > 55410 Benevolence
< _____ , ___ > 55420 Ben. Design: _____
< _____ , ___ > 55420 Ben. Design: _____
< _____ , ___ > 55470 Campaign Giving

Special Services:

< _____ , ___ > 55600 _____

Misc. Designations:

< _____ , ___ > (_____) _____
< _____ , ___ > (_____) _____
< _____ , ___ > (_____) _____
< _____ , ___ > 55590 Undesignated

_____ . ___ **Tithes & Offerings Subtotal**

MISSIONS

< _____ , ___ > 55530 Missions

Specific Missions Designations:

< _____ , ___ > 55535 _____
< _____ , ___ > 55535 _____

_____ . ___ **Missions Subtotal**

_____ . ___ **10550 TOTAL DEPOSIT** ⇔equal⇒

THIS WEEK'S OFFERING SUMMARY		
	Tithes & Offerings	Missions
Monday	$ _____	$ _____
Tuesday	$ _____	$ _____
Wed	$ _____	$ _____
Thursday	$ _____	$ _____
Friday	$ _____	$ _____
Saturday	$ _____	$ _____
Sun AM	$ _____	$ _____
Sun PM	$ _____	$ _____
Spanish	$ _____	$ _____
Total	$ _____	$ _____
		$ _____

Coin		Currency	
___1	_____.___	___1	_____.___
___5	_____.___	___2	_____.___
___10	_____.___	___5	_____.___
___25	_____.___	___10	_____.___
___50	_____.___	___20	_____.___
___$1	_____.___	___50	_____.___
Coin	_____.___	___100	_____.___
Cur.	_____.___	Cur.	_____.___
Cks	_____.___		
Total	_____.___		

_____
Counter's Signature

_____
Counter's Signature

Print Names of Other Counters: _____

_____

_____

Designations Itemized	
_____	$ _____
_____	$ _____
_____	$ _____
_____	$ _____

SEVEN

MINISTRY PLAN

You cannot read the story of Paul's ministry without being impressed that the man was following a determined course. Paul had a strong sense of purpose. Even when he was being a terror to the people "of the way," the man—then known as Saul—acted with purpose, doggedly going after that which he had determined to accomplish. As a saved man, Paul realized that he was no longer working alone but that Christ was the source of his strength. His words testify to this fact:

> *I can do all things through Christ which strengtheneth me. Notwithstanding ye have well done, that ye did communicate [partner] with my affliction. Now ye Philippians know also, that in the beginning of the gospel, when I departed from Macedonia, no church communicated with me as concerning giving and*

receiving, but ye only. For even in Thessalonica ye sent
once and again unto my necessity. Not because I desire a
gift: but I desire fruit that may abound to your account.
—PHILIPPIANS 4:13–17

Paul's determination was now channeled in the right direction and compelled by love for his Saviour. Paul's ministry life is a wonderful example of the truth of Proverbs 13:19: *"The desire accomplished is sweet to the soul."*

Until Christ returns, we too are to press forward toward the mark, motivated by our love for Him. To press toward the mark, we must have a mark and a plan for reaching it. Solomon counseled that we should have certain desires that we seek to attain. With the biblical desires God has placed in your heart, press forward. As the slogan admonishes, you must "plan your work and work your plan." There is nothing like accomplishing what you set out to do!

The ministry plan set out in this chapter does not constitute the only way to plant a church. Elmer Towns wrote a book in the mid 1970s discussing how ten different churches were started. (Fairfax Baptist Temple was chapter 3.) Basically, his point was that ten men used ten different ways to start ten different churches; yet each was successful in the beginning. So, the church planting experiences I discuss are not the only way to go about the work of church planting. I think, however, you will find some things that will work, or at the very least, things that you can modify to fit your specific circumstances and abilities.

I have been asked if the plan in this book applies on the foreign field. It actually depends on the specific country. I have been in over thirty-five countries, some in which these particular applications will not work. In some countries (mostly Islamic countries), "proselyting" or openly handing out tracts or preaching in the streets is prohibited by law. In some countries ten foot walls surround each house necessitating that the church planter adapt his methods. I am convinced, however, that with a little ingenuity, one can find a way to give out God's truth and start churches in most countries. I am reminded of Paul's efforts in Ephesus when he said, *"And how I kept back nothing that was profitable unto you, but have shewed you, and have taught you publickly, and from house to house"* (Acts 20:20). With a little imagination these principles will work anywhere.

MEETING PLACE

Much thought and prayer needs to go into every decision regarding the church plant. You must decide where God would have you work. Some of the men I've had the pleasure to train have known from the moment God called them where they were to go. This place was often a hometown or a place where they had lived previously (including foreign countries). Others have agonized in prayer over the decision for months. These church planters would travel to various places, asking God to impress upon them exactly where He was leading. Although a sending pastor might suggest some needy areas, it is important that the choice of location is made by the church planter. He must have complete peace about the matter regardless of what someone else may recommend.

Once you have decided on the state or country, and then the specific town or city, you need to look for a specific place within the community. Keep in mind the importance of your location.

People will form a first impression of your church by the location of your meeting place. There are some people that may never consider coming to your church simply because of its location. People who are lower on the socio-economic scale will often come to a middle class area, but the reverse is usually not true. I'm not saying that one class has more value than another. I am simply stating a fact that needs to be considered as you are searching for a place to hold meetings. If you are trying to reach middle class people but are meeting in a high crime or drug infested area, they will not come.

Assuming that the location is not a barrier to attendance, let's look at the next consideration. People will form an expectation about what they will find on the inside by what they see on the outside. They will make judgments about you and your ministry based solely on the condition of the building. If it's run down, it will give people an adverse impression. If it is neat and clean, it will give a favorable impression.

Try to see with an objective eye how things—inside and out—might look to a newcomer. A room full of junk, stuff piled on top of the piano, full wastebaskets, broken molding and light fixtures—these things just make a bad first impression and reflect negatively on the work of the Lord. You should work diligently on the appearance and cleanliness of the building, and immediately involve others in cleaning and otherwise preparing your facilities for church use. Examine each room for any details you can improve. Make it look as if you are always expecting company. Be particularly careful in the room you use for the nursery. You want it to be as clean and sterile as possible. (This advice also applies to those of us who have existing churches and facilities. First impressions are important!)

When you start out, there will be real limitations to work around. If, for example, you are renting a school building, you may not be able to make the room presentable by your standards, especially if the teacher is not careful about keeping the room neat. Nevertheless, you must be very respectful of the things the teacher has in the classroom. If the school children have projects in the room, you need to be careful not to disturb them and not to leave the church children unsupervised to get into those things. When you move anything, be sure to put everything back in its place when you leave each week. Anything that is found broken or out of place on Monday morning will be blamed on you, even in classrooms you may not be using! It only takes one complaint from one teacher to spoil your testimony, and one complaint may be reason enough for the principal to remove you from the school.

Another drawback you may face is promotional material on the walls of school buildings that are an absolute affront to Christian people. Similarly, if you are in other types of places, such as an Elk's lodge or VFW Hall, there are likely to be beer signs or even a bar area that you will have to work around.

There are many more things to consider than simply whether the room is large enough to accommodate sixty chairs comfortably. Evaluate carefully as you search for the right place.

It is not absolutely imperative that the building you use for your first week be the same one you use after that, but it is very helpful. Constancy starts to build stability—something that is not easy to come by when you don't have a permanent church building. You will undoubtedly have to enter into a rental contract for the space. While you want a contract long enough that you do not have to worry about finding new places all the time, you also want the ability to terminate the agreement if the place turns out to be unsuitable, or if, down the road, you find a permanent place to call your own.

If you can't buy your own facilities to start with (who can?), try to find a building that is easy to locate, one that is familiar to the community, in a location that is visible and that will allow you to put church signs out front, at least during the services.

Find a facility central to the people you want to reach. A public school is at the top of my list of recommended places. It is affordable, easy to locate, and easy to refer to. You will instantly have as many classrooms and restrooms as you need (though they will probably need your attention every week for cleanliness.). If you have your choice of rooms, consider a choral or orchestra room, which is often tiered and designed in a horseshoe shape so that you can see everybody and they can see you. Another benefit: these rooms usually have a piano. (Be sure that you have permission to use it; don't just assume.)

One disadvantage of schools, besides those mentioned previously, is that you will have to bring in the hymnals, offering plates, cribs, etc. each week to set up. When Fairfax Baptist Temple was young, we eventually secured the use of a janitor's closet for storage, but that doesn't always happen.

Another downside to using schools is that often they are unavailable for midweek services. This problem is probably true of many other locations used for other purposes during the week. When churches meet in schools on Sundays, they usually meet in someone's house for the midweek service. We met in different peoples' homes for three years. If you must do so, try to rotate homes.

Schools are usually less expensive than other places to rent initially, but that can change. In our county, the first year's rent is very reasonable. However, it escalates every year, and at about the fifth year, the rent escalates to an almost cost-prohibitive level. Also, you may find that the schools in your area are already full of churches. In our county, almost every school has a church of one type or another meeting in it. If only all of those men were presenting a clear Gospel message!

While a school is generally an ideal location, that option might not be available to you. Every area has different ordinances regarding the use of schools. Some forbid a church from meeting in schools even though they allow other organizations to use the building. This restriction may not be legal, but it is not a battle you can afford to fight. Also, the school principal may not be the one with authority to allow you into the building (though usually he is). You may have to go to the school board or the town council to try to get in. If a school is not available to you, then according to your budget, seek other alternatives.

A second place you might think about renting is a daycare center, which could also be a good situation for a new church. The owners are often kind and sympathetic toward your cause, and the set-up is great for your children. But there are some problems to think about. It may not have a large room well suited for your church service with adult-sized chairs and a piano you can use. You would have to acquire and transport chairs and a keyboard, in addition to the other things you would need each week. Also, the restrooms may be designed to accommodate children rather than adults.

Another idea is an industrial building. This may be suitable for a more permanent location. One of the men sent out from Fairfax Baptist Temple was in an industrial-style building for close to fourteen years before the church moved into a building of their own. However, the men of the church did a beautiful job of making the inside conducive for worship and fellowship. Industrial buildings are a little more expensive to rent, but you do not have to concern yourself with being put out of them. You can finish the interior so that it looks like a church, designing your own spaces for an auditorium, classrooms, and restrooms. A huge advantage is that you can set up your office in an industrial building. You rent or lease so many square feet; then you can go in and put up dividers where you want them. Since the zoning is different, you can usually get by with much more, and you may not be required to have a special use permit. On the downside, parking may be inadequate, especially where you need it, right in front of your space, and sometimes these buildings are not quite as visible as other public buildings.

Many of the men we have sent out recently have rented conference rooms in a motel. The advantages of these places are that they are generally in a very visible location and most people know where they are located. The drawback is that you will have many people wandering around in who knows what manner of attire. Also, the manager may reserve the right to bump you out if someone wants the room for a wedding, a Christmas banquet, or another high revenue-producing event. Parking may be tight at these locations too.

Consider using a storefront. It used to be very common for a church to move into a storefront. I still see them in some rural areas. Storefronts can sometimes be rented or bought depending on your financial condition. In small towns, downtown buildings are often available, prominent, and affordable. You would probably need to renovate the place once you moved in. One of our men rented an area in a strip-mall and built partitions, restrooms, classrooms, and an office in the space, and it looks great!

Regardless of what type of facility you rent or buy, never get something that is too big. Personally, I would rather be crammed into a classroom with fifty people than to be in a gymnasium with those same fifty people. I was told that when President John F. Kennedy held a press conference, he always found out how many people were coming so that he could hold it in a room that was too small for the anticipated crowd. Pictures on television or in print gave the impression that the conference was really important because of the overcrowded room. Conversely, if the room was too big, the pictures might give the impression that the event wasn't important enough for people to attend. In your church, a relatively small room will give a sense of oneness, and your people will feel the attendance growth as the room fills up.

Three rooms will usually be enough for the first few weeks or months of meetings. First, you will need a room for the nursery. Make sure you have one or more responsible mothers working. I recommend that early in the life of your church, you start a process of background screening your children's workers. The second room will house the preschool through sixth grade children for Sunday school. You will probably find that your wife is the ideal person to teach this class if there isn't anyone else. That room can then be used for children's church. The

VISION IS VITALLY IMPORTANT IN AN INFANT CHURCH.

third room is the main meeting room for teenagers and adults. As pastor, you will probably teach Sunday school and then use the same room to preach. As soon as you get qualified teachers and workers, you can start branching out, providing classes for teens, singles, senior saints, etc.

No matter what building you move into at the beginning, unless you are that extremely rare individual who has a permanent place from day one, you will need to emphasize that the facilities are temporary until you can locate some land and erect a building of your own. I would immediately start a building fund so that people can see that you are serious about securing your own facilities. Vision is vitally important in an infant church. For that matter, it is important in any size church.

PROMOTION

Once you know where your first meeting is going to be, have personalized invitations printed up. Make up a nice color brochure or flyer to announce the beginning of the new church. It needs to include the time and place, and the location shown on a map. Have a picture of the new pastor and his family along with a short biography of the pastor. Secure a post office box ahead of time to include for mailing purposes along with a phone number. Include the name of the sending church to let people know that you have many people behind this endeavor. Make sure that all material is printed on good quality paper and reflects first class design and printing. Nothing is gained by the appearance that you saved money on your print job.

Advertise in either the daily or weekly newspaper. The ad should be as large as you can afford and should reflect up-to-date graphics. Include all the same details noted above. Be sure to check the availability of free ads for new churches.

Many areas offer very affordable radio spots. I suggest going on a religious station. Most areas have at least one. It is best if you can go to the studio and record the spot yourself. This way you can convey warmth and love to your new community with a personal touch rather than have a stranger from the station read the ad. I would check on free church service announcements as well by going in to meet the radio station manager.

Have as large a portable sign as you can have out on the road. If you are meeting in a large school, you may also need signs in the parking lot pointing to the right door to use. Signs may also be necessary in the hallways.

I recommend that you plan to "blitz" the community with literature advertising the new church (and then monthly after you have begun). A minimum of six to eight weeks ahead of the actual starting date, you will need the material for the door hangers in hand to give you a couple of weeks to assemble them. Also, you will need to line up people from your home church and other supporting churches who will be ready to do the stuffing as soon as you have all the material. This is not a one-week project. It takes many people working many hours. (Note: put the most colorful item you have on the outside so that it is visible in the door hanger bag.) Preprinted Gospel tracts are necessary, and you may want to use a Gospel of John and Romans or another booklet. Everyone throws away "junk mail" but people are less inclined to throw away a Bible or portions of it. There are churches that print these as a ministry, and you can purchase them rather inexpensively, possibly with a custom-designed cover. I recommend putting these materials in a clear plastic door-hanger bag to pass out around the community.

I suggest handing out twenty to thirty thousand of these door hangers before the first meeting. Obviously, this number is determined by the number of volunteers you have and the size of your community, but keep in mind that "...*He which soweth sparingly shall reap also sparingly; and he which soweth bountifully shall reap also bountifully*" (2 Corinthians 9:6). If your budget allows, you might mail out a number of these announcements as well.

Print out prospect cards and color-coordinated maps to be used by the visitation/blitz teams. Start in the area closest to your meeting facilities. Highlight enough streets to have approximately 150–200 homes on each map (keep the maps so you can use them again later). There are many variables that determine how many houses someone can cover in a two to three hour time frame, including weather, the kind of housing (apartments, single family homes, farms), the terrain (steps and hills take longer than flat areas), etc.

When you set about the task of hanging the plastic bags on the doors of homes in your community, you may meet with some resistance. Some may try to tell you that you have no legal right to do it. They are wrong. The U.S. Supreme Court has stated that this activity is regarded as protected free speech. Some may argue that you are violating "no solicitation" signs. You are not. Your activity is leafleting. You are not selling anything. However, if you are confronted, you must be respectful.

Though you have every right to leaflet, you must obey the regulations and restrictions that are in place. If there is a "no trespassing" sign on a property, then you must honor that. (You may want to mail the literature to these addresses.) The courts have ruled that no trespassing signs on private property bar your right to enter. Also, do not put the bags in mailboxes or hang them from mailbox flags or on the posts.

THE NEW PASTOR'S RESPONSIBILITY

Finish your personal and church budgets (discussed in chapter 6). Take account of how much support you have from your sending church and how much you need to raise from other churches. Consider your own savings and assets. Don't be afraid to use those if necessary, but be careful about wiping out all of your savings, particularly if you are older.

Consider whether or not you have sufficient funds before beginning. When you feel you are financially prepared to get started, set up a bank account for the new church with a local bank. This is a good time to introduce yourself to the banker since you may need his assistance in the future.

If your sending church can't help much and you're having a hard time getting others to help, you may have to get a full-time or part-time job to help support your family. Some of the men we have sent out have found it necessary to work a secular job when the support commitments come to an end.

Remember, if you, as a minister, have opted out of the self-employment tax, you still have to pay FICA and Medicare from your secular work. Also, if you have worked at secular employment for a while before planting the church, you may want to ensure that you have completed the minimum number of quarters to qualify for Social Security benefits. There is no point in losing the benefit if you are close to achieving it.

Locate housing. It is usually best to rent when you first move. This may be your only option unless you are selling a home before you relocate. Before you settle on permanent housing, you want to make sure you buy in the proximity of where you plan to build your church. Because you may not know the location immediately, renting is wise in the beginning.

Once you have these details settled, make sure that you have sufficient life, health, and homeowner's or renter's insurance. You may want to check on liability insurance for the new church.

Communication is an area you don't want to overlook. Before the first week of services, you should have your church stationery ready along with a well written, grammatically-correct template letter that you can personalize and send to every visitor who attends your services. One of the worst things you can do when planting or maintaining a church is to fail to recognize and thank visitors. Make sure you have all of your signs ready to go, and check on the radio and newspaper ads. Have a church-specific email account. You want people to be able to contact you easily if they have any questions about the new church.

Also, be sure to contact the pastor of any church of like faith and practice in the area to let him know you are coming into the community and to assure him that your purpose is not to take his members. It is likely, however, that members of other local churches of like faith will attend your services. To protect your reputation,

> THERE IS NO SUBSTITUTE FOR KNOWING YOUR BIBLE.

communicate with the pastor about those people. Remember, you are not competing with the other pastor; you want to work in concert with him to evangelize the community.

It is essential for you and the sending pastor to coordinate your starting date as early as possible, allowing the members of the sending church who are considering going to help with the new church plant to clear their calendars for that time.

As you prepare for your ordination, keep in mind that there is no substitute for knowing your Bible. It is mandatory! If you are still nervous about *"rightly dividing the word of truth,"* don't start your church yet. Wait until you have a better handle on the Word of God.

RECOMMENDATIONS FOR THE SENDING PASTOR

The new pastor's ordination service needs to be coordinated with the sending church and put on the schedule. Encourage your church family to attend the examination, but limit those doing the questioning to ordained ministers and deacons. Upon the recommendation of the ordination council, present him to the congregation for a vote, and then have a special service on a Sunday evening.

A few months prior to the time the new pastor is to leave the sending church, take a special offering to be used by the new pastor for his start-up costs: literature, hymnals, offering plates, communion set, office supplies, keyboard, and a host of other items. Announce to the church family that the new church plant is an official project of the sending church and that you are receiving tax-deductible donations on behalf of the new church. People are often willing to supply many of the items the new church will need to get started.

When the time comes for the new pastor to leave, have the commissioning service, usually the week before, as a special event for the sending church and the new pastor and his wife. Take the time to make sure that everyone in your church is acquainted with this couple and their plans. This is also a good time to introduce all the people who are planning to help with the first week of meetings.

Remind the church of their responsibility to pray for and support this couple and the new church. You might want to preach a message that night on the importance of what your church is about ready to do—give birth to a baby church. It is a good time to take another special love offering for the new pastor, as he will have a lot of personal expense associated with the move and setting up his new home.

Sending Pastor, in my opinion your involvement in starting this new church is worth your missing a Sunday back home. This event needs your help and visible support, and your presence will encourage the new pastor. When you return home, be sure to share the excitement with your church family. Give a personal testimony, and have others who went give testimony of their experiences. Show pictures if you have them.

Stay in weekly contact with the young pastor, and let him know that you are praying for him. Ask him how many doors he knocked on that last week. Keep him accountable to you at least until the time that the new church has its organizational service. Plan on attending that service.

I suggest that soon after the church has begun, usually three to six months after the beginning, you plan a charter-signing service. Some men like to wait until they have a substantial number of potential new members (25–50), but I wouldn't wait too long. Some churches are several years old before they even have twenty-five in attendance! There isn't a right or wrong in the matter, but prudence tells you that operating as an official church is better than prolonging the wait until you have a particularly large number to sign the charter as members. Ideally, fifteen to twenty is a good number.

The following is a sample of what this charter looks like (items that may not apply in every situation are in brackets):

Charter

Fairfax Baptist Temple

of

Fairfax Station, Virginia

December 6, 1970

We the undersigned, having received Jesus Christ as Saviour
and Lord of our lives, having been baptized by immersion,
having read carefully the Constitution [and Bylaws], and
being led as we believe by the Triune God, do hereby
constitute ourselves a duly organized independent Baptist
church, FAIRFAX BAPTIST TEMPLE, Fairfax Station,
Virginia, and to this end do hereby affix our signatures.

Like giving birth to a child, giving birth to a church has
its moments of joy and disappointments. It has its ups and
downs. No question about it though, the joys far outweigh the
disappointments! It is a labor of love to be repeated time and
time again.

THE FIRST WEEK

The following passage, in describing the expansion of the first century church, gives testimony that the first week of a new church plant is one of the most exciting adventures of a pastor's life.

> *And from Miletus he sent to Ephesus, and called the elders of the church. And when they were come to him, he said unto them, Ye know, from the first day that I came into Asia, after what manner I have been with you at all seasons, Serving the Lord with all humility of mind, and with many tears, and temptations, which befell me by the lying in wait of the Jews: And how I kept back nothing that was profitable unto you, but have shewed you, and have taught you publickly, and from house to house, Testifying both to the Jews, and also to the Greeks,*

*repentance toward God, and faith toward our Lord Jesus
Christ. And now, behold, I go bound in the spirit unto
Jerusalem, not knowing the things that shall befall me
there: Save that the Holy Ghost witnesseth in every city,
saying that bonds and afflictions abide me. But none of
these things move me, neither count I my life dear unto
myself, so that I might finish my course with joy, and
the ministry, which I have received of the Lord Jesus, to
testify the gospel of the grace of God.*—ACTS 20:17–24

Church planting is phenomenal! It is such a tremendous
blessing. I still love to go back and think of those early days,
and your early days will be memorable for you too. They are
foundational to what will follow in the years to come.

A few things come to my mind when I look at these verses,
the first being the *attitude* we are to have—one of humility. We
should always approach the Lord's work with a heart of humility.
Whatever happens, it is from the Lord, and He deserves the credit
and glory. Whether ten or one hundred attend your first service,
praise the Lord! Also foundational to the work of the ministry
are our *actions*. Notice the action of this new church. They went
from "*house to house.*" I can't emphasize enough the importance
of a church (young or old) sticking with the biblical method of
door-to-door evangelism. As Paul addressed the elders, he also
mentioned the inevitable *afflictions* he would be faced with. For
the new church planter these might include disappointments,
lack of finances and workers, and a myriad of other trials.
Regardless of the afflictions, if the new church planter will keep
his attitude right and be faithful in his actions, his afflictions will
pale in comparison to the joys of being a church planter.

It is important to always remember that God's work is just that—God's work, not ours. In Acts 20:28 the Bible says, *"Take heed therefore unto yourselves, and to all the flock, over the which the Holy Ghost hath made you overseers, to feed the church of God, which he hath purchased with his own blood."* Humanly speaking, you are the man who abandoned your prior occupation, uprooted your family, moved to an area where you know no one, wore out three pairs of shoes going from door to door, scoured the area for a place to meet, and erected a sign announcing to all the world that the "New Baptist Church" is open. But it is the Holy Ghost who has appointed you to the office of pastor. And, while you are the public face of New Baptist Church, you are not its head. *"And I say also unto thee, That thou art Peter, and upon this rock I will build my church; and the gates of hell shall not prevail against it"* (Matthew 16:18). The church is built on the Rock. Jesus Christ is the head. We are His servants, doing His will at His beckoning.

> THE CHURCH IS BUILT ON THE ROCK. JESUS CHRIST IS THE HEAD. WE ARE HIS SERVANTS, DOING HIS WILL AT HIS BECKONING.

Paul viewed his life this way. Notice a few things in Acts 20:19. Paul's *manner* was to serve the Lord *"with all humility of mind."* He was humble, realizing the wonderful privilege it is to be one of God's servants. Paul's *method* was to go from house to house. There are some who will try to tell you that, in our modern day, door-to-door visitation is not worth the effort it takes. I disagree strongly. No method is more immediately effective in giving out the Gospel message than standing face to face with someone on his doorstep and asking him if he knows with certainty that he will go to Heaven when he dies. Many people will not want to engage you in that conversation, but some will. Whether they do or not, their eternity hangs in the balance.

I have a mindset that has kept me knocking on doors for forty years. Rather than approach soulwinning with the idea that I am going to take a person from spiritual indifference to salvation at our first meeting, I go with the expectation that the Holy Spirit will lead me to the door of a man in whose heart the Holy Spirit has already been working, convicting the man of sin and righteousness and judgment. I view myself as having a God-directed appointment with that man. Regarding the others I meet, I plant seeds or water seeds with the hope that perhaps some day I, or someone else, will reap a harvest there. So, whether I am planting seeds, watering, or enjoying the privilege of harvesting, my mindset is that I am cooperating with the Holy Spirit of God in His work.

You have sent out your mailings. You have done the Gospel blitzing. You have taken out newspaper and radio ads. All of these are good, but none of these require a man or woman to answer directly the most important question of life: Have you accepted Jesus Christ as your Saviour?

To those of you who send out missionary-evangelists or are a missionary-evangelist yourself: I have had several conversations with men who try to convince me that God's method of door-to-door visitation does not work in their country. "You can't get to the door because of the gated courtyard." "There are no doors or doorbells on these huts." "It's too dangerous to walk the neighborhoods." Many are the excuses people give for not doing God's work in God's way. There is no excuse sufficient to justify neglecting God's Word.

Door-to-door visitation is meeting people where they live. The point I want to make clear is that you have to get out where the people are. In the United States, that means going to the home. In other places, it may mean that you spend a lot of time in the marketplace. If the culture of the place in which you minister dictates such, it ought to be that when you walk through the marketplace, you are greeting people by name because you have spent time there cultivating friendships. Making opportunities for personal conversation between friends is important, especially in the "restricted access" countries where there are strict legal impediments to evangelism. You must go where the people are if you are going to touch them with the Good News you are there to give.

Paul's *message* was one of repentance toward God and faith toward our Lord Jesus Christ. To repent is literally to have a "change of mind." Man has to recognize his sinful state and ultimate separation from God. *"But your iniquities have separated between you and your God..."* (Isaiah 59:2). After learning of God's holiness and man's sinfulness, one must change his mind about his own condition and about who God is, and he must accept what the Lord has done for him. Just changing his feelings is not enough. God wants man to put his faith and trust in Him. Faith is expressed by placing trust in the Gospel or the good news that Jesus died and rose from the grave (Romans 10:9; 1 Corinthians 15:3–4). Some have a tendency to generalize the Gospel. It is biblically defined as the death, burial, and resurrection of Jesus Christ. Christ is no longer in the grave! He is alive! Giving out the Gospel is giving out the message of hope.

Paul's *motivation* is clear. He said, *"I go bound in the spirit unto Jerusalem"* (Acts 20:22). His work was something he had to do. You too must have passion. If your passion dies, you will willingly follow the many distractions that entice you away from God's work.

> GIVING OUT THE GOSPEL IS GIVING OUT THE MESSAGE OF HOPE.

This work has to be your life. Just as a mother understands the sacrifices she must make to bring a new life into this world and to care for her new baby, you must understand that it takes work, dedication, and passion to birth a new church. If the church planter doesn't have the conviction that this work is God's will for his life, he will fail miserably because, at times, this work can be discouraging. But remember, Pastor, you can never afford the distraction of discouragement.

Armed with the right manner, method, message, and motivation, roll up your sleeves and get ready to meet your first week of new ministry.

BUILD EXCITEMENT IN THE SENDING CHURCH

This should be an extra special week for the members of the sending church as well as for the pastor of the new church. There is nothing quite like giving birth to a baby church. It is thrilling!

The sending church can and should help with as many of the expenses and needs as possible. They can also help by assembling a "church planting team"—normally thirty to sixty people—made up of families and individuals who are willing to distribute literature and attend the first services at the new church. This will be a good opportunity for their soulwinning training to be put to practical use.

This opportunity should be open to as many as would like to go from the sending church—singles, teens, and entire families. If the plant is scheduled for summer, take a whole group of teens with you. They will be a great blessing, and the experience will challenge their spiritual lives as well as nurture lasting friendships among the team. Just being around a brand new church environment is exciting! You never know, someone on the team may even be called into the Lord's work as a result of the experience.

Give the dates of the first services as early as possible so that people can request time off from their jobs. Have some meetings ahead of time with this group to develop camaraderie. Do what you can to encourage a "team spirit" and build excitement.

Instruct the group about what to expect. Everyone going to help should be expected to take care of their own expenses and motels. For their own comfort, remind folks to come with comfortable shoes and loose but not baggy clothing. Dress should be conservative and modest. Be specific about dress guidelines so that there are no surprises. For the Sunday morning service at the new church, everyone should dress according to the expectations that you will set for the church from the beginning.

BUILDING RAPPORT WITH AREA PASTORS

Two to three months prior to the actual week of meetings, the sending pastor and new pastor should try to travel to the location of the new church specifically to meet with pastors of churches of like faith within about a thirty-mile radius of the new church. It is simply a matter of good ethics to introduce yourself to other like churches and let them know what you are doing. The new pastor could visit the area pastors individually or invite them for a meal at a local restaurant to meet them all together. The goal is to get the area pastors excited about having a new church in the community.

If you choose to assemble the pastors, it would probably be best for the pastor of the sending church to share the similarities of your churches. There is no sense in even mentioning any points of distinction between your churches because you may be perceived as antagonistic, and your purpose would obviously be defeated. Sadly, some may see the new pastor as a competitor rather than as a fellow servant and will be looking for anything to validate those feelings.

Establish trust and demonstrate respect by letting them know upfront that you have no intention of adversely affecting their ministries. Their big concern is that you might "take" some of their members. Put the pastors at ease by indicating that your goal is to go after lost and unchurched people.

Sending pastor, let them know that you, as the sending church, have commissioned the new pastor to start a church in this particular area. At this point, let the new pastor ask for their help in starting this new church. New pastor, you will want to let them know that you are looking for joint participation if they care to help. Solicit their direct help in going door-to-door prior to the first service. (If the local pastors tell you that door-to-door doesn't work in that community, don't argue the point. Just tell them that you are distributing bags of information.) Make yourself available to share your work with their church family if they are interested.

BUILDING A RELATIONSHIP WITH THE COMMUNITY

There are a couple of ways to conduct the activities of the first week. One way is to have one or two "get acquainted" nights on Friday and/or Saturday before the first Sunday. In doing this, the local pastors could participate by having some of their people help with the music, ushering, or greeting for the get acquainted meetings. A note of caution: You should not allow another area church to supply music during your introductory meeting, or at the first Sunday meeting, unless you know that their music philosophy is compatible with yours. Involve a different church each night, and try to include the pastor to encourage, pray, or welcome the visitors.

Having these introductory meetings is helpful to draw a crowd together so that the people who are interested in attending your church won't feel like they are the only ones in attendance. The added crowd will also help to convey the idea that something is happening, and it is!

The other way—the way we currently start a church out of the Fairfax Baptist Temple—is to eliminate the weeknight services and start with the Sunday morning Sunday school and church service. Our experience has been that this is just as successful in getting people out, and it gives those who go door-to-door all day a good respite in the evenings.

The team from the sending church should show up on Wednesday afternoon or evening of the week that the church will start, unless they are within close driving distance, in which case, they could make the trip on Thursday morning. We work with our church planting teams from Thursday through Sunday, allowing ourselves enough time to distribute twenty to thirty thousand door-hangers. If you have a small team, you may want to get your people to take off the whole week and start on Monday or Tuesday to get the task accomplished. On Wednesday night after arriving, you, as the sending pastor, could gather your people together to attend another church in the area, or you could have a special prayer meeting with the new pastor.

On Thursday morning at 8:30 AM, everyone should assemble at a designated place, like a park with picnic tables. Ask the new pastor to bring a devotional to share his heart for the new work as well as to express his personal thanks for each one who has come to help.

The new pastor should then hand out assignments to everyone. He should have already made up prospect cards and color-coordinated maps showing the streets to be covered, making sure that the directions from the assembly area to the assigned neighborhoods are specific. To avoid wasting time, the new pastor should be very familiar with all the maps so that he can give explicit instructions on how to get to each area. He must have the pick-up points and time expectation worked out so that everyone knows what to expect. Every group needs a cell phone (in case someone gets lost) and plenty of water.

Your goal as the new pastor introducing yourself to the community is to get the information about your church to as many houses as possible. Therefore, there is no need to knock on doors. Instruct the teams on what to do as they go out blitzing. Typically, all streets should be covered by pairs (one on each side). Several teams of two could be dropped off to cover a specific area. In most cases, they will simply hang the bag on the doorknob and go on to the next residence. If they find people in the yard or at the door, they should introduce themselves, explain what they are doing, and invite them to come to the introductory meeting (if you are having one) and especially to the first Sunday morning service. From the people who show interest, they need to get the name, address, and telephone number on a prospect card to give to the new

> PASTOR, YOU CAN NEVER AFFORD THE DISTRACTION OF DISCOURAGEMENT.

pastor for follow-up at a later date. If they are reluctant to give out their information, teams should nonetheless make a note of the address for the new pastor.

The teams should all return to a central place for lunch. We normally take about one hour for lunch and fellowship. Maybe a few ladies will not go on the blitz so that they can fix sandwiches to have ready when the teams return. Buying food is another option. Take care what you feed the people. A good number of them may not be used to the physical exercise, and you don't want them sluggish from eating junk food. Also, make sure that everyone gets plenty of hydration and rest before going out again. After lunch, most people will be able to go out for another couple of hours.

You can follow the same schedule Friday and Saturday. The whole experience is a tremendous training time for everyone. You're doing the will of God, and that is exciting! It is exciting for everyone who participates to know that they are part of something God is doing. It builds interest in witnessing and soulwinning as well, which will have lasting benefit on the sending church when these folks return home. It strengthens one's faith and increases one's boldness for the Lord.

For the new pastor, it should be noted that although this kind of Gospel blitz is good, it is not a substitute for literally knocking on doors to give the householders an opportunity to hear personally about the salvation Jesus offers. At our home church in Fairfax, we have a Gospel blitz one Saturday a month, but on the other Saturdays, we have an organized effort to knock on every door in our area.

BUILDING ANTICIPATION IN THE NEW CHURCH

For the first Sunday morning service, make sure that the rooms you are using give the appearance that you have prepared. Chairs should be straight with hymnals and visitor cards out. Everything should be clean and neat, including bathrooms.

Have the order of service—special music, DVD, etc.—planned and ready to go.

On Sunday morning, the sending pastor could share a few words of welcome, introduce the new pastor, and tell about his relationship with him. Pastor, make sure the people know that the sending church is 100 percent behind the new church. You should exude excitement about this new church beginning! It should be nothing short of a spiritual pep-rally!

In fact, everyone involved should ask God to help them create and demonstrate a spirit of excitement and anticipation. The group of people that have come to help could be used as greeters, ushers, nursery workers, musicians, altar workers, and clean-up crew, but the most important thing they will do is interact in a very friendly way with the visitors. They are not there to converse with their friends from back home. Rather, they should go out of their way to engage visitors in conversation, answer any questions they may have, and try to introduce them to the new pastor. They should also be instructed to be very attentive during the service, not moving around or causing any distraction for those visiting. Remember, the prospective members don't know who is a visitor from their community and who is not.

It is good to have some light refreshments set up for fellowship after the service to encourage an atmosphere conducive to conversation and relationship building. God *is* going to work. It will be a wonderful, enjoyable time.

It would be nice if everyone from the sending church would be able to stay through both services on Sunday. There should be a time of celebration that evening. No matter what the outcome is, you can still find cause to celebrate just knowing that you are serving the Lord and working for God.

Praise the Lord for the blessings of God! The Wednesday after the new church plant, the sending pastor should consider having as many team members as possible share a testimony. They could recount what they saw God do and how they were affected personally. The purpose is to rejoice together and to create excitement so that the next time you send out a church planter, everyone will want to go help. All of this will help to kindle excitement for church planting and for sending out another man of God and his family.

A FINAL WORD

Not every area is the same. Some churches start up like a mushroom, growing quickly. Others don't. The typical scenario is that you may have disgruntled people from another church, backslidden people, curious people; and every now and then you get some that are energetic and looking for something to be a part of, to be involved in, and to help establish. Whichever kind of area you are in and whatever you face, if you follow these procedures, they will help you get the new church underway.

NINE

GRACE GIVING

This chapter discusses how churches raise money specifically for their missions program. The alternatives are to set apart a portion of the general budget or to have a separate missions budget. I wholeheartedly recommend a separate missions budget.

Keep in mind that when I speak throughout this chapter of "grace giving" for missions (church planting), I am referring to not only foreign missions but also home missions. I have suggested that your intern program for preparing, training, and sending out church planting pastors or missionary-evangelists is also appropriately funded this way. At Fairfax Baptist Temple, about 70 percent of the offerings designated for missions is earmarked for monthly support of both our foreign and domestic missionary-evangelists and pastors. A portion of the money is also dedicated for our intern program. It pays the salary of the intern while on staff, and it funds the church planter's first year or two of support so that the man does not have to worry about feeding his family while working to get the church growing.

As I discuss funding world evangelism, I use the terms *faith promise* and *grace giving*. For many years, dating from before the 1970s, the idea of "faith promise" was promulgated as a means to provide for the missions budget. I prefer the term *grace giving*. The ideas are similar, but I think that *grace giving* is closer to the language of the Bible. These terms are defined and contrasted in this chapter.

GOD'S PLAN FOR FUNDING HIS OBJECTIVE

Jesus spoke more frequently about money than He did about Heaven or Hell combined. He even referred to money more than to His Second Coming. Aside from being an interesting bit of Bible "trivia" (is anything in the Bible trivial?), this recurrent mention of money advises us that the way we manage the money God entrusts to us is spiritually significant. While I never cared to know what any of the members of Fairfax Baptist Temple gave in the offering plate, I did ask our deacons who counted the money to visit families if they decreased their giving or ceased to tithe, because giving is always a barometer of the heart. A decline may indicate a spiritual problem in the family that needs to be fixed.

Just as negative changes in giving habits may indicate a spiritual problem, positive changes may reflect spiritual growth or maturity in the life of a believer. Spiritual maturity manifested in giving is exactly what we read about in 2 Corinthians 8:1–7:

> *Moreover, brethren, we do you to wit of the grace of God bestowed on the churches of Macedonia; How that in a great trial of affliction the abundance of their joy and their deep poverty abounded unto the riches of their liberality. For to their power, I bear record, yea, and beyond their power they were willing of themselves; Praying us with much intreaty that we would receive the gift, and take upon us the fellowship of the ministering to the saints. And this they did, not as we hoped, but first gave their own selves to the Lord, and unto us by the will of God. Insomuch that we desired Titus, that as he had begun, so he would also finish in you the same grace also. Therefore, as ye abound in every thing, in faith, and utterance, and knowledge, and in all diligence, and in your love to us, see that ye abound in this grace also.*—2 CORINTHIANS 8:1–7

GIVING IS ALWAYS A BAROMETER OF THE HEART.

Though God has clearly mandated the local church to go into all the world to preach the Gospel, many churches seem to have forgotten this objective, or at least they have put it on the "back burner," failing to pursue it wholeheartedly. It is so easy to get caught up in the "me" generation philosophy without realizing that when we concentrate our efforts only on our own church, we have allowed this philosophy to permeate our beliefs and practices. Every pastor and church need to get a global vision if they are to emulate the burden of our Heavenly Father: *"For God so loved the world, that He gave His only begotten Son…"* (John 3:16).

Since God so marvelously designed the strategy that world evangelization be through church planting, He also prescribed a financial means for carrying out His objective. This financial plan is often referred to as *faith promise* or, put in more biblical terminology, *grace giving.* This giving is nothing more than God funding His program through His people in His churches. In other words, our giving is based on our faith in *His* ability. We simply need to ask ourselves, "How big is our God?"

It is my understanding from the study of Scriptures, that there are two kinds of grace giving referred to in 2 Corinthians. The first kind, which I just touched on, is grace giving through faith (better known as faith promise), and the second kind is grace giving through generosity, which we will discuss later in the chapter.

GOD'S PROMISE TO GENEROUS GIVERS

I remind us that grace is always attendant with blessings from God. We know the Bible says that we are saved by grace: *"For by grace are ye saved through faith…"* (Ephesians 2:8). Grace is unmerited, undeserved favor that God makes available to all mankind: *"For the grace of God that bringeth salvation hath appeared to all men"* (Titus 2:11).

Paul said in 2 Corinthians 8:1, *"Moreover, brethren, we do you to wit of the grace of God bestowed on the churches of Macedonia."* This grace denotes the grace of giving and seems to be the theme of chapters 8 and 9 where the subject is brought up many times, in verses 8:1, 8:6, 8:7, 8:9, 8:19, 9:8, and 9:14.

A direct relationship between a church's missions program and God's gracious blessings on that church exists in the wonderful promise made in Philippians 4:19: *"But my God shall supply all your need according to His riches in glory by Christ Jesus."* Many of us have claimed that verse, but consider, in all honesty, to whom this promise is made. A careful reading of the context will reveal that the Apostle Paul was commending the church at Philippi for their continued supply of his needs as a church planter.

> *Now ye Philippians know also, that in the beginning of the gospel, when I departed from Macedonia, no church communicated with me as concerning giving and receiving, but ye only. For even in Thessalonica ye sent once and again unto my necessity. Not because I desire a gift: but I desire fruit that may abound to your account.* [This is good missionary philosophy] *But I have all, and abound: I am full, having received of Epaphroditus the things which were sent from you, an odour of a sweet smell, a sacrifice acceptable, wellpleasing to God.*
> —PHILIPPIANS 4:15–18

In other words, Paul was saying to the church at Philippi that because they had so often been generous by giving to his needs as a church planter and helping him on his journey, they could be assured that God would supply all their needs. Not every Christian and church can claim that promise—only those sacrificially involved in missions giving.

When our church had outgrown its facilities and the five acres we were on, we started looking for more property on which to relocate. Unfortunately, no one was making any more land in the Fairfax area of Washington, D.C., and most of what was available was either too far away, too small, or too expensive; but we had several people looking regardless!

One of our men came to me and said, "Pastor, I know we have a missions conference coming up where you will be encouraging people to give more to missions, but you might want to back off a little because we are going to need a lot of money if we are ever going to get a new piece of property." There was no question in my mind that this person simply wanted to help by reminding me of the big picture. After hearing that, however, I became more determined than ever to promote increased giving to world evangelism, and I did. We had the largest commitment to missions that year than any other year prior.

About a month later, one of our deacons, Mark Edwards, who was also a land developer, told me he had found a piece of property he wanted to show me. We went to look at the 33 acres about four miles from our present location. It was beautiful, except for one problem–it was on Pohick Road! I could just hear the imminent remarks about our church being a bunch of "poor hicks." He dismissed my doubts, noting that a four-lane divided highway would be built to replace Pohick Road and there would be a major intersection at the corner.

About a week later on a Wednesday night in the church lobby, he told me that his research had revealed the property was available and we simply had to put a deposit on it the next day to enable us do a study on it for six weeks. I must have looked shocked at the moment, as I imagined myself walking into the auditorium to tell the people, "We just found a potential piece of property,

> IF YOU TAKE CARE OF GOD'S BUSINESS (WORLD EVANGELISM), HE WILL TAKE CARE OF YOURS.

and we need to pass the offering plates again so we can all give tens of thousands of dollars tonight to secure the contract!" I thought, "No way. I'm not a miracle worker!"

Mark then asked me if he could see me in my office. When we were alone, he asked, "Do you really think this would be a good property on which to relocate?"

I told him, "Absolutely, but I can't just walk in there and spring this on them on such short notice. Furthermore, I know we can't afford it."

He said, "Well, suppose I put down the earnest money and then buy the property myself and give it to the church!" I almost fainted!

As it turns out, he bought the property and gave it to the Fairfax Baptist Temple. It went on the books at the Fairfax County courthouse for over three million dollars.

I will believe until the day I go to Heaven that the reason God worked it out for us to get our property free was because we, as a church body, were very generous with our grace giving toward worldwide church planting. From this situation, I developed a little philosophy: if you take care of God's business (world evangelism), He will take care of yours. Paul said, in effect, "Philippians, since you have been so generous in meeting all of my needs while I have been out starting churches, I want you to know that my God will supply all your needs." There is a timeless principle that, if we fully understand it, will change our attitude toward funding world evangelism. Here it is: if we are good missions givers, then we are justified in claiming the promise of Philippians 4:19. Because our church was giving to missions and world evangelism, God gave us the property we needed.

GOD'S PRINCIPLES FOR GIVING

WE ARE TO GIVE REGARDLESS OF OUR PROBLEMS.

Notice what 2 Corinthians 8:2 says regarding the Macedonian churches: *"How that in a great trial of affliction the abundance of their joy and their deep poverty abounded unto the riches of their liberality."* They were in a great trial. We find here a principle of grace giving: God expects us to have an open-handed attitude even when our financial situation is tenuous.

Don't wait until you get everything worked out to give. If that is the way you operate, the devil will always put something in your way to hold you back. You must learn to give in the midst of your trials—even if they are financial. Has it occurred to you that your economic woes may be a God-appointed test of your spiritual maturity? By the way, that is exactly what the word *trial* means: "putting to test" our faith. Trials prove us to be whom we claim to be in Christ. My prayer is that God will never have to impose deep poverty on me to prove that I have the same dependent faith as did those people.

WE ARE TO GIVE IN POVERTY OR PROSPERITY.

We are to give—*even* in our poverty, I might emphasize. Poverty is a relative condition. In a third-world country, poverty means something entirely different from what it means in the United States. Some people in America think they are in poverty because they have only a one-car garage instead of a two-car garage! Second Corinthians 8:2 uses the phrase *deep poverty* to describe the Macedonian churches. These people were experiencing significant physical deprivation, yet they abounded in their giving.

While Paul is writing here about actual physical poverty, I believe it does no violence to the text to contrast financial health with spiritual health. Look again at 2 Corinthians 8:1–2. "*Moreover, brethren, we do you to wit of the grace of God bestowed on the churches of Macedonia; How that in a great trial of affliction the abundance of their joy and their deep poverty abounded unto the riches of their liberality.*" The direct result of their giving attitude, even in the midst of great physical poverty, was abundant spiritual riches pinpointed in one word—*joy*, a pleasurable emotional response arising from inner peace despite the hardships of day-to-day life. Spiritual joy is the overflowing of an already full heart.

These churches were experiencing the joy of fellowship that comes from co-laboring with Christ.

In our Saviour's letter to the church of Laodicea, we are presented with the antithesis:

> *Because thou sayest, I am rich, and increased with goods, and have need of nothing; and knowest not that thou art wretched, and miserable, and poor, and blind, and naked: I counsel thee to buy of me gold tried in the fire, that thou mayest be rich; and white raiment, that thou mayest be clothed, and that the shame of thy nakedness do not appear; and anoint thine eyes with eyesalve, that thou mayest see.*—REVELATION 3:17–18

The Laodiceans were as far from the deep poverty of the Macedonian churches as one can get. With their abundance of earthly wealth, however, came a deep spiritual poverty: *"thou art wretched, and miserable, and poor, and blind, and naked."* Jesus knocked outside the bolted door of the Laodicean church, desiring to come in and fellowship. But the churches of Macedonia, through their generosity, out of their poverty, had swung open wide this door of fellowship.

WE ARE TO GIVE IN POWER.

Notice 2 Corinthians 8:3. *"For to their power, I bear record, yea, and beyond their power they were willing of themselves."* Please notice two areas of giving: *"to their power"* and *"beyond their power."* To our own power is what we know we can give. It's based on what we think we can work out by ourselves. Beyond our power is where "faith promise" giving comes in. It is based on God's ability. Most people don't think about God's ability when they commit to missions giving. I think many make up their minds about what to give as an academic calculation rather than as a passionate spiritual decision.

Once again, Paul reminds us that these principles all begin in the heart when he notes that *"they were willing of themselves."* Their

> TRIALS PROVE US TO BE WHOM WE CLAIM TO BE IN CHRIST.

giving was in all ways voluntary and joyful, proceeding from the riches of their collective hearts. The Macedonian churches made a spiritual decision to give sacrificially. They were greatly involved in church planting—specifically Paul's ministry of church planting. In 2 Corinthians 11:9 Paul again gives account of their sacrifice:

> *And when I was present with you, and wanted, I was chargeable to no man: for that which was lacking to me the brethren which came from Macedonia supplied: and in all things I have kept myself from being burdensome unto you, and so will I keep myself.*—2 CORINTHIANS 11:9

Paul made it very clear that the Macedonian churches helped him time and time again. This kind of giving went beyond their power, yet it cost them something to give this way. Grace giving should cost us something as well.

GOD'S PEOPLE IN COOPERATION

Notice that in 2 Corinthians 8:5 the apostle writes, "*And this they did.*" The giving was something they were *all* involved in voluntarily. While each member of the local church body must make an individual spiritual decision, it is important to look at the effort of the church as a whole. Giving is contagious! I know from having heard many testimonies over the years that people are motivated to give when others around them are giving, which is why I believe the apostle was telling the church at Corinth what the churches in Macedonia were doing. When we see or hear about others stepping out in faith, it encourages the rest of us to grow in this grace also. There is a combined exuberance when everyone does his part for the Lord.

Preachers, we should do everything we can to build a culture of world evangelism into the backbone of our churches and into the very fiber of our people. The last chapter sets out twenty-one suggestions for having a dynamic missions conference, but the annual, or biannual, missions conference is just one way for the people of your church to get to know the front-line warriors in the battle for souls raging beyond the doors of the local church. Each church gathering should be a happy place in which the Holy Spirit has free course to work in everyone's heart. The people should have a spirit of anticipation, wondering who will be the next young (or old) man to be called into the ministry of church planting somewhere in the world, or who will be the next young lady to go into the Lord's work. Everyone, regardless of his calling, should participate in grace giving for missions.

Giving is something we are to "abound" in as stated in 2 Corinthians 8:7. "*Therefore, as ye abound in everything, in faith, and utterance, and knowledge, and in all diligence, and in your love to us, see that ye abound in this grace also."* Paul made it clear to the people that they were doing a good job of abounding in everything including their faith, their witnessing, their earnestness in learning Bible truths, their diligence, and their love, which they so freely expressed to Paul and his companions. He further urged them that, with the same passion, they

GIVING IS CONTAGIOUS!

were to excel in the grace of giving. This was not to be a tacit agreement or some tip of the hat toward world evangelism. Rather, they were to take to heart the importance of giving, knowing the end of their giving would be glorifying God in their obedience and furthering world evangelism.

GOD'S PREREQUISITE FOR GRACE GIVING

Here is the key to the missionary problem, or most any church problem for that matter: we are first to give our *"own selves to the Lord"* (2 Corinthians 8:5). The complete verse states, *"And this they did, not as we hoped, but first gave their own selves to the Lord, and unto us by the will of God."* As preachers, we should assume the burden of encouraging our members to give themselves wholly to the Lord. Once our people understand biblical stewardship of their lives and material goods, involvement in world evangelism will be easier. I have never cowered at preaching and teaching about giving, especially missions giving, because I know that if I can somehow encourage others in giving, *they* will be blessed. It is for their good and growth! And, of course, more money will be available to help church planters get to their field to plant more churches for the glory of God.

So God wants us to take our hands off our own lives, including our wallets, and realize it all belongs to Him. We have only one life, and we are to make it count for God. He is looking for people who have a heart for Him and care about lost and dying souls in the regions beyond their local community.

Take another look at 2 Corinthians 8:5. *"And this they did, not as we hoped, but first gave their own selves to the Lord, and unto us by the will of God."* The second part of verse 5 is often overlooked. It is a good thing for every member of the church to consider the importance of caring for and helping the pastor and other leaders of the church. God blessed the Macedonian churches for doing so, and I am convinced that He will bless our churches if we have a heart to give ourselves to the ministry and to the pastors for the work of the ministry.

I think it is only appropriate at this time for each of us to look into the innermost recesses of our hearts to see if we are, in fact, given over to our Lord. There is no question that time, as we know it, is short. What we will do for our Lord we need to begin now.

ANOTHER LOOK AT GRACE GIVING

When teaching grace giving by faith, or "faith promise" giving, preachers typically tell individuals to get alone with God and ask Him to put on their heart an amount beyond their own ability that they can trust Him to provide. While I appreciate this emphasis on faith and the leading of the Holy Spirit, I want to challenge you to also lead your church family in a more planned and intentional approach to grace giving.

In reality, most Christians (me included) wind up giving an incremental increase each year to reflect growth and progress. In the following divisions, I propound what I believe to be a second way of giving by grace, in addition to or in place of the "faith promise" approach. I call this "grace giving through generosity" or "grace giving through sacrifice." Here is something all of us can understand and practice!

A CALL TO GENEROUS GIVING

Early on in my ministry, I preached a message on giving. Having had little experience in preaching this subject, I studied extensively to be as thorough as I could and basically preached everything I knew on the subject of giving. After I finished preaching and concluded the service, one of our members, Brother Gil Hansen, came bounding up to the platform to greet me in his usual enthusiastic manner. Leaning on the pulpit, he looked me in the eye and declared with a smile on his face, "Pastor Calvert, I was just thinking. Jesus Christ had His 'Sermon on the Mount,' but you have your 'Sermon on the A-mount!'" Please allow me to submit what I learned from this study, what I believe to be a thrilling addition to our discussion of biblical giving.

Remember that 2 Corinthians 8–9 are dealing with grace giving, the first kind being "faith promise," which Paul describes in verses 1–7. Earlier, the Apostle Paul had stated that faith promise was giving "*to their power*" and then "*beyond their power.*" In other words, they made a financial commitment that would be impossible barring the intervention of God. His point is clear. The people gave as they did despite their deep poverty because they had faith that God would supply their needs. They genuinely practiced what we would call "faith promise" giving.

Faith promise is a commitment beyond anything I could possibly do myself. When I give by faith, it isn't necessary to consider my income or financial status because I am depending, not on my ability to give, but on God's ability to give through me monies that He will provide. My commitment is based on my faith in His promise to provide for those who give to further the work of world evangelism, and it demonstrates that my faith lies not in what I already have coming in, but in what I believe God will supply. I might, for example, commit money based on my faith that God will bless me so that I make more sales, do more business, earn more money, have less repair needs, come by an inheritance or a bonus, receive an unexpected gift, make money on the sale of my house, etc. or that God will provide in some other unexpected way.

While we talk about faith promise giving, the reality for the vast majority of us is that we do not give to God on the basis of faith, promising God that we will give a committed amount and trusting Him to provide it even though we do not know how He will place the money into our hands. In the great majority of cases, the way we give—the way that I give and the way I suspect you give—is a programmed or planned way. I know today exactly what portion of my next paycheck—the percentage above my tithes—I plan to give toward missions (and also the building program and my personal "others" fund) just as I know what portion is allocated for my mortgage, food, and clothing. In other words, I have not really promised by "faith" anything. My giving is actually planned, programmed giving. If this is how you give as well, what is the relevance of God's instruction to us in 2 Corinthians 8, the classic passage used to teach faith promise giving?

I believe that practicing planned, programmed giving over and above the tithe demonstrates an accurate understanding of the Word of God. I'll explain that statement as we progress through the passage; let me begin with 2 Corinthians 8:7: *"Therefore as ye abound in every thing, in faith, and utterance, and knowledge, and in all diligence, and in your love to us, see that ye abound in this grace also."* What is "this grace" that Paul has in mind? It is the grace that Paul also mentioned in verse 6: *"Insomuch that we desired Titus, that as he had begun, so he would also finish in you the same grace also."* It is the grace of giving. It is the grace of giving with a heart that is acting in accordance with divine influence. It is the grace of giving materially after a person has given self over to the Holy Spirit. Paul urges that we would *"abound in this grace."*

The *dominant* theme and exhortation we find in 2 Corinthians 8–9 is a call to "abounding" giving. Paul is trying to help us see the importance of being generous in our giving. He is not merely asking us to set aside a little extra to help with a special need. Rather, Paul is essentially saying, "The need is now. Whatever you do, be generous."

This whole section of Scripture is dealing with generous, liberal giving. Having lived in the Washington, D.C. area for most of my life, I have heard much about liberals and conservatives. I used to think that life would be so much better if we could dispose of the liberals somehow. Now, having a better understanding of my Bible, I know that what all our churches need is a bold fresh number of liberals—liberal *givers* that is!

As we continue through 2 Corinthians 8, we see several aspects that instruct us on the heart we must develop toward grace giving.

THE EAGERNESS OF THE MACEDONIANS

"*I speak not by commandment, but by occasion of the forwardness* [eagerness] *of others, and to prove the sincerity of your love.*" The "others" he mentions here are the churches in Macedonia to whom he had referred earlier. He clearly acknowledges the eagerness of the churches at Philippi, Berea, and Thessalonica but at the same time makes it clear that he is not commanding anyone to be a generous giver. This kind of giving comes not from pressure but from a heart of love.

Verse 8 contains a simple love test. The word *prove* in this verse implies an opportunity to demonstrate by evidence. The Macedonian churches passed the love test with flying colors by demonstrating great sacrifice and generosity in the throes of extremely difficult economic times. I have always thought how easy it is to sing "O How I Love Jesus" but how difficult it is to show how much I love Jesus. Jesus didn't say that if you love Him, you should regularly sing about Him. Rather, He said, *"If ye love me, keep my commandments"* (John 14:15). I believe God is looking for a little sacrifice from us to help with the needs of others.

THE EXAMPLE OF CHRIST

Although the gracious givers of the Macedonian churches were held up as an example, they are not to be the standard against which we measure ourselves. Who is the proper measure? Paul tells us that it is none other than Christ Jesus Himself. He is the standard of grace giving. Second Corinthians 8:9 says, *"For ye know the grace of our Lord Jesus Christ, that, though He was rich, yet for your sakes He became poor, that ye through His poverty might be rich."* Here we see the self-sacrifice and self-impoverishment of God's Son on man's behalf. This verse encapsulates the extravagance of Christ's love and gives us the supreme argument for Christian generosity.

Paul explains our Saviour's selfless giving more fully in Philippians 2:5: *"Let this mind be in you, which was also in Christ Jesus."* What mind? It is the mind of selflessness and servitude that characterizes Christ.

Every Christian will profit from examining his heart regularly to discern his priorities and values. I read years ago that if a man wants to find out what is important to him, he must simply look at his checkbook register. In it he will discover where he allocates his treasure: credit cards, mortgages, school bills, savings, and automobiles. None of these things are necessarily sinful, but each item seems to disclose what he values financially and often reveals his lifestyle.

The Bible says, *"But lay up for yourselves treasures in heaven, where neither moth nor rust doth corrupt, and where thieves do not break through nor steal: For where your treasure is, there will your heart be also"* (Matthew 6:20–21). God's assessment is this: where your treasure lies is where you can find your heart's interests and loves. Perhaps we should be seeking to lay up more in Heaven by facilitating world evangelism through the local church. My wife and I decided many years ago that our largest monthly investment would be our offering toward starting churches through our church's missions program.

As is often the case in life, it is quite easy to find some worse-off, less-blessed, out-of-favor-with-God person with whom to measure ourselves. There is bound to be someone we can find who is less spiritual and therefore less generous than we are! It is so foolish, however, to compare ourselves with any one else other than Jesus Christ. He simply gave His all.

THE EXPEDIENCE OF THE COMMITMENT

Paul reminds the Corinthians of their former commitment to help with the need that the Jerusalem saints were experiencing:

And herein I give my advice: for this is expedient for you, who have begun before, not only to do, but also

to be forward a year ago. Now therefore perform the doing of it; that as there was a readiness to will, so there may be a performance also out of that which ye have.
—2 CORINTHIANS 8:10–11

These people had learned of the need on Paul's previous visit, and now he is asking them to fulfill their promise.

This situation resembles our yearly missions conferences in that the Corinthian church committed to help meet a need just as many modern churches commit to help meet the needs of church planting. We challenge people each year, sharing with them the needs of more missionary-evangelists who are anxious to get to their respective fields.

ANOTHER KIND OF GRACE GIVING

Paul reminds the Corinthians in verse 10 of the commitment they made and encourages them to follow up. In verse 11 he says that God wanted them to bring to fruition their intended purpose. Margret Thatcher, former Prime Minister of England, stated, "No one would remember the Good Samaritan if he'd only had good intentions—he had money as well." I'd say that it is not so much that he had good intentions and money, but that he did something good with them. He acted on his good intentions. Paul promotes exactly the same deportment in this passage. He encourages another kind of giving in which he urges the Corinthians to give out of that which they have, with hearts of love, following Christ's example of extravagant giving.

We see it in the last part of 2 Corinthians 8:11: *"Now therefore perform the doing of it; that as there was a readiness to will, so there may be a performance also **out of that which ye have**"* (emphasis added). Here Paul advocates the kind of giving that I call "grace giving through generosity." While faith promise is based on belief that God will provide, grace giving through generosity commits "out of that which one has." One might ask, "How could this be? They seem contradictory."

As I read this chapter, it seems to me that Paul is making a distinction (whether intended or not). Although he told the church of Corinth about the giving of the Macedonians and the hardships under which they gave, he didn't tell the Corinthians to give like that. Perhaps their economy was different, or perhaps Paul realized that, because they were having so many personal problems, their faith wasn't as strong. So rather than challenge them to give by faith as the Macedonians had, he suggests to them to dig down deep and give generously out of that which they had. This would be what is often called a "sight" offering as opposed to a "faith" offering. The truth of the matter is they are both good ways to give!

Giving "out of that which ye have" is further explained in verse 12, which says, *"For if there be first a willing mind, it is accepted according to that a man hath, and not according to that he hath not."* The test of a man's generosity is not based on income or wealth; rather, it is based on his willing mind.

Grace giving through generosity is a commitment to give according to what you have. It is sitting down with your budget, looking at your gross income and saying, "Ten percent is the tithe; 20 percent is extracted by the government. I am committing to God to give an additional x percent, and I will live on what remains." You do this because you have a mind that places a priority not on self but on giving to the work of the ministry. Purposefully, I have not used a number in the example

because suggesting a number is not for me to do. The amount that you give is a matter that is settled between you, your spouse if you are married, and your God.

THE TEST OF A MAN'S GENEROSITY IS NOT BASED ON INCOME OR WEALTH; RATHER, IT IS BASED ON HIS WILLING MIND.

I remember reading a story about a country preacher who was going out to visit one of his members who, like many others in the church, was a farmer. The preacher drove out to his place and saw the farmer out in back of the barn. After a little small talk the preacher said to him, "Jake, I would imagine that if you, being the godly man that you are, had two farms like this one, you would probably be willing to sell one and give the proceeds to the Lord at our missions conference next week."

"Yeah, preacher, if I had two, I reckon I would be willing to make the sacrifice and sell one to give the proceeds to our Lord for church planting."

"Jake, if you had two of these tractors, would you be willing to sell one of them and give the proceeds to missions?"

"As God is my witness, if I had two of these tractors—and this is a good one—seeing that our missions conference is here, I would be willing to sell one and give the Lord all I get for it."

"How about a hog like that? If you had two of them, would you be willing to give one to the Lord's work and keep just one for yourself?"

"Now, preacher, you know I have two hogs!"

All of us can look at someone who has much more than we do and think, "If I had his wealth I would be willing to give tens or hundreds of thousands and just keep a million for myself!" It's always easier to say I would be generous if I had more money than to be generous with the money I have right now.

I probably shouldn't put this in a book, but...I used that story in one of my messages one time when I was preaching in a country church in Senoia, Georgia. When the pastor and I were driving from the airport to his church, I noticed the farm land in his town and the farm equipment out in the fields. So, when I came to the part in the illustration about the two tractors, I thought I would make it a little more personal and name the kind of tractor it was since these country folks would know exactly what I was talking about.

EVERYONE CAN BE GENEROUS AND SACRIFICIAL—THIS IS WHERE THE EMPHASIS SHOULD BE WHEN RAISING MONEY FOR WORLD EVANGELISM.

"Jake," I said, "if you had two of those concubines, would you be willing to give one to God and keep just one for yourself?"

I thought I had said *combine* but obviously I had mispronounced it! The unfortunate part was that, although the people laughed, I didn't know why until about fifteen minutes later when I was giving the invitation! (In case you are wondering; yes, I am a city boy!)

God is not concerned about what you would do if you had money or wealth. He is concerned about what you are doing with the stewardship you do have.

Preacher, I have been in many churches and missions conferences, and I can tell you that the vast majority of Christians have a hard time relating to giving from that which they don't have—by faith. In my opinion, most Christians, especially in difficult economic times, can more easily relate to looking at their budget or income and making sound financial decisions based on what they see happening the next year. Since no one knows the future, even this kind of giving has an element of faith. Everyone can be generous and sacrificial—this is where the emphasis should be when raising money for world evangelism.

Paul continues the subject of giving in verse 13:

> *For I mean not that other men be eased, and ye burdened: But by an equality, that now at this time your abundance may be a supply for their want, that their abundance also may be a supply for your want: that there may be equality: As it is written, He that had gathered much had nothing over; and he that had gathered little had no lack.*—2 Corinthians 8:13

This passage makes it clear that everyone can be involved in world evangelism because God has provided sufficient resources for the people He has gathered together in our local churches. The Macedonians gave in deep poverty; the Corinthians gave of their abundance. Every church can be actively and generously involved in supporting church planting activities worldwide. The problem is not that God has not funded His work. The problem is that His people are not using His money for His best purpose.

What is His best purpose? What is the heartbeat of God? He wants every person, no matter where he lives on this planet, to come to faith in Him. World evangelism is the heartbeat of God. Since that is what He cares about, that is what each of us ought to care about as well. How is your heart? Does it beat in synchrony with God's?

NO REGRETS

Years ago Mary and I were making a four-country tour of Central America, visiting some of our missionaries. One of our stops was Guatemala, the "land of eternal springtime." We were in a beautiful city of over 1,000,000 people. After a service one night, my wife and I decided to take a walk and asked the missionary, "Is there any place we shouldn't walk?"

He responded, "You should be safe anywhere, but here's my calling card in case you get lost." I wasn't planning on getting lost for two reasons: one, I was in an Airborne Reconnaissance platoon when I served in the United States Army so I am familiar with landmarks and navigation techniques, and two, I am a man, and men don't get lost! Occasionally, we get misdirected or a little disoriented but the situation is never serious enough to warrant asking for directions!

To make sure I wouldn't need his card, we turned right out of his front gate, walked two blocks, turned right again, and walked another two blocks. Then we turned around and started walking back. As we strolled along, we noticed that, as in most Latin American countries, all the houses were surrounded by eight to ten-foot walls with glass imbedded on top to discourage any one from climbing over. Most of their gates were closed. A few cars had passed by intermittently, so I didn't think much of it when we heard a motorcycle come from behind and slow down. Naturally, I thought it was a neighbor getting ready to pull into his driveway, but the motorcyclist pulled right up beside us, and the man said, "Buenas noches."

WORLD EVANGELISM IS THE HEARTBEAT OF GOD.

I actually ignored him and without looking at him continued walking, because I don't speak any Spanish, and I was afraid he would try to engage us in conversation. I would be unable to do anything but smile in ignorance! He repeated, this time rather indignantly, "Buenas noches."

Mary and I in one motion stopped and turned to respond with "Buenas…." Before I could say anything else, I realized I was looking down the end of a gun barrel pointed at me! Two men were on the cycle, one driving and the other holding the gun. Living in the Washington, D.C. area all my life, I had gone through the mental exercise of what I would do if someone tried to hold me up. I decided that since no amount of money is worth one's life (especially mine!), I would give them all the money I had. However, traveling overseas is different; I always put my passport in my wallet so that I don't chance losing it. I instantly thought, "I can't give this guy my wallet. It has my

passport, and I won't be able to catch my plane in the morning."
So I shouted with out-stretched hands, "I don't have any" and
ran as fast as I could. At that point, I turned around and ran
back to get my wife, and then we ran together! No, actually I
didn't leave her the first time. We ran back about two houses
where I remembered seeing the gate was open, and we dashed
in and knocked on the door to see if we could use their phone.
Yes, I had to use the card after all!

As we were lying in bed that night contemplating our
escape, thanking God he hadn't pulled the trigger, we asked
ourselves if there would have been any regrets had we been
shipped back in a box. Had we given God all we could give? A
little philosophical thought came to me: "Live for God today,
and there will be no regrets tomorrow."
I know it is not a Scripture verse, but it
is a scriptural principle.

> LIVE FOR GOD TODAY, AND THERE WILL BE NO REGRETS TOMORROW.

As Christians, we will some day
have to give an account of our lives
and stewardship to our Lord. Thank
God we will not be giving an account
of our sins because they were washed
away with the precious blood of
Jesus Christ. But we will give an account for what we do in this
lifetime. *"Every man's work shall be made manifest: for the day
shall declare it, because it shall be revealed by fire; and the fire shall
try every man's work of what sort it is"* (1 Corinthians 3:13). What
determines whether a man's work will survive the purifying
fire of God's judgment? It is the attitude of his heart when he
performed it. For this reason Paul wrote, *"Every man according*

as he purposeth in his heart, so let him give; not grudgingly, or of necessity: for God loveth a cheerful giver" (2 Corinthians 9:7). Certainly we can all give above our tithes to help the cause of church planting through our church missions program. May God help us to do our best for Him today while there is time.

How do you discern an amount that is acceptable to God to give through your local church so that the church is able to send out church planters? I suggest that you look to Christ's example of giving, and with a heart of love, dig deep. May you *"abound in this grace also."*

TEN

MISFORTUNES

I n Romans 10:1–4, Paul expressed the great burden he had for the Jewish people.

Brethren, my heart's desire and prayer to God for Israel is, that they might be saved. For I bear them record that they have a zeal of God, but not according to knowledge. For they being ignorant of God's righteousness, and going about to establish their own righteousness, have not submitted themselves unto the righteousness of God. For Christ is the end of the law for righteousness to every one that believeth.—ROMANS 10:1–4

Moses also expressed so great a burden and love for his people that he was willing to die for them. The burden these men carried should become the paradigm for every pastor and missionary. May we always keep in mind that the ministry is first and foremost about *people*—people for whom Christ died. As our Lord gave Himself for us, so we must give ourselves for the people to whom He has given us to minister.

Though the outcome of our labors is not always what we wish for, the fear of God compels us to continue going after men. Not everyone in the churches that Paul started and pastored were fully sanctified; he, nevertheless, continued to put people in the forefront of his endeavors. He said, *"Knowing therefore the terror of the Lord, we persuade men…"* (2 Corinthians 5:11).

As a safeguard to himself in serving in the various churches he said this:

> *Therefore seeing we have this ministry, as we have received mercy, we faint not; But have renounced the hidden things of dishonesty, not walking in craftiness, nor handling the word of God deceitfully; but by manifestation of the truth commending ourselves to every man's conscience in the sight of God.*
> —2 CORINTHIANS 4:1–2

Notice three important things he said here. First, Paul had determined that he wasn't going to quit. *"…We faint not,"* he stated resolutely. Men of God, you need to keep in mind that the difficult, trying times will come, but they should simply remind you that Satan is at work and increase your resolve to see God build His church!

Second, I bring to your attention that Paul *"renounced the hidden things."* In other words, he did a continual "heart check." He realized that though others were unable to see what was hidden in the recesses of his life, God could. Therefore, he eliminated the hidden things that displeased God, and in so doing, he was able to proclaim the Gospel with a pure heart. There may be things in our lives that must be renounced for us to continue forward with a clear and pure conscience.

Third, to keep himself from falling prey to the "misfortunes of the ministry," Paul made it a point to live by and preach the truth of the Bible. Just as the Corinthians could see Christ in Paul's life, so people should see Christ in us who profess Jesus Christ to be our Saviour. Paul said very clearly to the church at Philippi, "*...so now also Christ shall be magnified in my body, whether it be by life, or by death. For to me to live is Christ, and to die is gain*" (Philippians 1:20–21).

THE MINISTRY IS FIRST AND FOREMOST ABOUT PEOPLE.

The Apostle John commended Gaius for the truth manifest in his life: "*I rejoiced greatly, when the brethren came and testified of the **truth** that is in thee, even as thou walkest in the **truth**. I have no greater joy than to hear that my children walk in **truth**"* (3 John 3–4) (emphasis added). It is one thing to know the truth, God's Holy Word, but an entirely different thing to walk in it. May we all be "*doers of the Word and not hearers only...*" (James 1:22).

Most of you have spent four years in Bible college preparing for the work of the ministry. Some, more. Now it is lab time—time to see if what you have been taught really works. Can it be done? A better question: *Will* it be done? To answer that question, you must first answer this: Can I *live* what I have learned, or will I suffer some of the misfortunes of the ministry and fail?

Many things can stand in the way of churches starting and succeeding. What are these misfortunes that severely hinder or even stop the work of God?

LACK OF BIBLE PREPARATION

I think that everyone will agree that before starting a church, the new pastor should understand God's Word and its doctrine. The truth is that no one starting out, if he thinks soberly about his God-given responsibility to care for and feed a congregation, will ever feel that his knowledge is deep enough. After thirty-five years in the office, I have discovered that there is always something more to learn about God as the Holy Spirit reveals Him through His Word.

This unveiling of truth is a fathomless well from which the preacher can draw to teach his congregation. It also keeps the work of Bible study and sermon preparation fresh as the man works on three messages each week.

The Bible does not set as a requirement that the pastor be an accomplished theologian from day one. The standard is set out in 1 Timothy 3:6: *"Not a novice, lest being lifted up with pride he fall into the condemnation of the devil."* There has to be time for the newly converted man to learn how to handle God's Holy Word.

There is, however, a long distance between the novice and the scholar who spent years of study to earn a master's or even a doctorate degree—if institutional degrees are sought. During that period of growth there is no reason that a man should not do the work of church planting.

No matter what his background entails, every man of God must acquire a good foundational understanding of Bible doctrine. Meeting the biblical standard of *"not a novice"* can be accomplished in a number of ways, only one of which is Bible college or seminary. Self-directed study (1 John 2:27), which includes reading quality authors and being under sound preaching, affords a beneficial path toward understanding sound doctrine. Even better is when the home-church pastor offers an internship so that he can challenge the intern's thinking and help him increase in knowledge. As far as the "how to" is concerned, the sending pastor can use the internship to make sure the future church planter is familiar with all the church planting concepts mentioned in this book.

LACK OF INFORMATION

By this I mean that it is possible to have a desire to start a church, but not the know-how to start a church. I have seen some very sincere and biblically literate men set out to start a church only to fall flat on their faces simply because they did not know what to do. Failure resulted, not because they did not have the heart to do the work, but because they did not have a plan or the head knowledge necessary to get the church off the ground. Starting a church takes not only a great effort but also much understanding about the "how to."

Romans 10 (at least in part) refers to the Jews' desire to serve God, but it was a desire that was *"not according to knowledge."* They had a zeal for God, but it was not biblical zeal. They therefore served Him their own way, a practice that never works. *"For I bear them record that they have a zeal of God but not according to knowledge"* (Romans 10:2). Note that they were at least sincere, but sincerity is not enough for the work of God, which takes preparation, planning, purpose, and perspiration.

I would not doubt the sincerity of any church planting pastor or sending church, but sometimes their methods hinder their work. Perhaps neither the new pastor nor the sending pastor is familiar with church planting methods and concerns. The sending church itself may be stepping into unfamiliar territory as it sends out a church planter and, due to inexperience, is unable to give adequate direction. Perhaps the sending church is running so smoothly that the church planter thinks that he can just "wing it," though he is not fully prepared for his new ministry. I submit to you that if you don't know where you are going, you'll probably get there quickly!

Most men, whether going to the mission field or staying in their home country, would benefit from an internship in their home church to better understand how the ministry works. For those going to a foreign country, it would also be of great value to work alongside a veteran missionary for about a year to get acquainted with the culture, language, and customs. This experience will greatly enhance the missionary's strategy for going about to start churches.

The inexperience of the church planter—even one whose sending pastor has not had experience in starting a church—is not a problem as long as he familiarizes himself with the ins and outs of starting a church. Prospective church planter, you can gain this information by reading this book and others and by talking with those who have started a church. They can give you many helpful insights about selecting a location, advertising the first week, planning the first budget, and setting up procedures for handling finances. It would also be very helpful for you, as the new pastor or sending pastor, to go with someone who is starting a church to see how they do it. Try to spend that first week with him passing out door-hangers and asking as many questions as you can. Perhaps contact some churches that have started other churches to find out if they have any new ones planned for a time when you might be able to go with them.

LACK OF FAITH

Since faith is *"the substance* [to stand under] *of things hoped for, the evidence* [proof or conviction] *of things not seen"* (Hebrews 11:1), it is essential in the church planting process to have explicit trust in the Lord. As we all know, the common thread that binds all the great men and women in the Christian "hall of fame" (Hebrews 11) was their faith. These people had such strong and real faith that they exercised it all the way to the grave.

Starting a church has to be accomplished by someone who stands firm on the conviction that this is what God wants him to do and, therefore, he can do it. The faith has to be *his*, not the sending church's faith or anyone else's. As with any decision of great importance, spending time alone in fasting and prayer would be a very prudent exercise for the church planter. Man of God, make sure of your calling (evangelist or pastor). Six months after you start is no time to be wondering if God meant for you to be an assistant pastor some place!

Back when I first started our church it was popular to say, "Give, until it hurts." Today, however, people hurt too easily and give up too quickly. Paul understood pain: *"We are troubled on every side yet not distressed; we are perplexed, but not in despair; Persecuted, but not forsaken; cast down, but not destroyed"* (2 Corinthians 4:8–9). Even amidst his suffering, Paul demonstrated his confidence in faith. Having listed his trials, he referred to the faith of the psalmist in Psalm 116:10 and stated that he too had this faith, *"We having the same spirit of faith"* (2 Corinthians 4:13). The church planter must stop at nothing. His faith is that which keeps him going in the midst of trial and doubt. In short, I reiterate Paul's words: *"Having done all, to stand. Stand therefore…"* (Ephesians 6:13–14).

Disappointments will come—your nursery worker didn't show up; people promised you they would attend, but they didn't; the money didn't meet the budget; the attendance was low; you spent extra hours preparing a message you knew would help people who didn't come—and when disappointments come, it is easy to start questioning your call and God's plans. That is exactly what the devil wants you to do.

Often it becomes necessary for a new pastor to work an outside job to provide for his family. When that is the case, he should work diligently toward becoming self-supporting from the church. Pastor, don't hesitate to let the church know of your plan and goal (time-table) to become fully supported by the church. And when the time comes, step out by faith without hesitation. I remember when my wife, my son, and I went to Fairfax to start the Fairfax Baptist Temple; I had worked up a budget, and my full-time salary was going to be (I hate to date myself!) $85 a week. To make sure I got my salary the first week, I put in $100 that I had received from the sale of our house trailer. It was a step of faith, but God has met our needs the whole way. And He will bless your faith too.

LACK OF FINANCES

This goes right along with what I said in the previous paragraph about finances becoming a matter of faith. It is unfortunate when there is not enough money to begin or continue a new church. No missionary should go to the field under-supported, and no pastor should start without counting the cost. The sending church should prayerfully and financially do whatever they can, which should equate to sacrifice and commitment. But often the sending church lacks commitment, possibly as a result of its own financial struggle. Pastor, if you are going to send someone out, make sure you stand behind him. This endeavor is certainly costly, but it's worth it!

The new pastor needs to "press toward the mark" regardless, not allowing finances to stand in the way. After discussing with his pastor what the sending church can do to support him, the new pastor may want to go on deputation, or attend some preachers' meetings to let the men know what he intends to do. Some of their churches might like to support him.

In my opinion, although it is tempting, it is best for a new pastor not to solicit money from individuals other than family members. Church planting is a church responsibility, and we should not let expediency stand in the way of doing things God's way.

Along with raising support, the new pastor needs to sit down with his wife and work out what the late Grant Rice called a "survival budget," proving their willingness to sacrifice.

LACK OF FAMILY SUPPORT

Although church planting cannot take place without a God-called pastor, let us not forget the importance of his wife. She must be in total agreement. (Notice the word *total*.) If she gets discouraged or is not really supportive, the church planter will never make it. I am simply saying that the ministry is a "we" proposition. When a church gets a pastor, they get his family too.

We understand just how important the family is to the man of God from the biblical warning that one can disqualify himself from the ministry because of his family. Pastor, if your children are not *"in subjection with all gravity"* (1 Timothy 3:4), you disqualify yourself from the ministry. If you are not ruling and leading your own home for the Lord, once again, you disqualify yourself from the ministry. Thank God for every God-fearing wife and child in our families.

It's not necessarily easy to live in a preacher's home. I am not the first to say it; everyone knows that the preacher's wife and children live in a "glass house" or "fishbowl." That is, they are on display for all to see and criticize because people place higher expectations upon pastor and missionary families. By the way, no one is without faults, but be careful about using your wife and children in a negative illustration just to get your point across. It's difficult enough to live in a "fishbowl" without your pointing out their faults to the whole congregation.

Make it a policy never to talk about your wife in a negative context. In fact, it is a good idea to demonstrate your love for your wife openly. I want everybody to know that I love my wife, and I shared that regularly from the pulpit. On our twenty-fifth wedding anniversary, I gave my wife a new diamond ring on the platform in front of everyone. Although we pastors are mere mortals, it is possible for a woman in the congregation to elevate a pastor to a pedestal he does not merit, believing he would be the ideal, if not "perfect," husband. It is a regrettable misfortune when pastors, unaware of their environment, become

> THE MINISTRY IS A "WE" PROPOSITION. WHEN A CHURCH GETS A PASTOR, THEY GET HIS FAMILY TOO.

vulnerable to the *"wiles of the devil."* Conveying your love for your wife openly will help to keep the devil away and will let others know how madly in love with your wife you are. Keep in mind that if you lose your marriage, you have no ministry.

When I first started in the ministry I heard other pastors suggest or come right out and say that you shouldn't go on a vacation or even take a day off because the ministry demands your all. I actually believed that for a day or two! However, I since found out that you can't have a viable ministry without the support of your family, and you won't have a family if you constantly neglect them. As I said earlier, "Don't make your wife a widow while you are still alive!" Don't neglect her because you are so important and busy. Make time for her. From the time I first started our church, I always took Monday off to

> **IF YOU LOSE YOUR MARRIAGE, YOU HAVE NO MINISTRY.**

spend with my wife and son, and we reserved Friday night for family time as well. It is possible to lead a healthy church and maintain a healthy family at the same time. Friend, be sure to make your family your first priority after your relationship with God. Always strive for the right balance, even when starting a church.

In chapter 7, I made mention of your wife working with the children, and I need to expand on that for a moment. Men, be particularly careful how you treat your wife. I shared with Mary in the very beginning that her main responsibility was simply being my wife and the mother of our son.

Every pastor's or missionary's wife should be involved in the church, just as you would expect every other woman in the church to be, but she doesn't necessarily have to lead the various ministries. My wife, Mary, was my first secretary, children's teacher, ladies' teacher, soloist, and pianist (a position she held for thirty-five years)! She was also involved in many other ways.

In the beginning, your wife will need to help with the nursery and children's class, and if she is musically inclined, she might play piano or sing. In fact, she may wear many hats— receptionist, secretary, counselor, soulwinner, and a myriad of others. It would be prudent, however, to start delegating some of these things to others as soon as you can. Let her enjoy being a wife and mother, as well as a Christian servant. Start as soon as possible training others for the "work of the ministry."

There should be no closer couple working together than the man of God and his wife. Pastors and evangelists, what a great privilege it is to have a God-fearing wife by your side! Thank God for this relationship, and do all you can to nurture it.

LACK OF FIRE

It is always a sad scenario when the starting pastor does not have the fire or passion needed for starting a church. I am reminded of what Paul said: *"For though I preach the gospel, I have nothing to glory of: for necessity is laid upon me; yea, woe is unto me, if I preach not the gospel"* (1 Corinthians. 9:15)! Now that I have been out of the pastorate a few years and have been in many other churches, I can testify that it is also a sad scenario when an older pastor has lost his fire and passion.

The ministry is not an 8:00 AM to 5:00 PM job; it's a 24/7 commitment. It is a calling on a man's life. It takes mind, body, and soul to minister for God. Many times on my day off I would have to handle an emergency—whether a counseling phone call, a hospital visit, or a family need—and I was glad to do it. It is a wonderful trust to have this God-given ministry. It is a great privilege to have people call you "Pastor."

"And whatsoever ye do, do it heartily, as to the Lord, and not unto men" (Colossians 3:23). There is little worse in the work of God than the sin of laziness. We must have God's power to accomplish His work, but having power is going to take a diligent prayer life, a disciplined walk with God, and consistent Christian living. These are absolutely essential for all of us.

I remind you that Satan's full-time job is to try to douse the fire in your soul. That's a given. Realizing Satan's strategy, never let down your guard for any reason. Stay in the Word, stay on the firing line, stay red-hot for God!

The Fairfax Baptist Temple has always been a church full of leaders—God-fearing men and women who give 110 percent to whatever they do. Many have a love and devotion for our country and work day and night to keep America safe. I commend them for their service. As ministers of the Gospel, we too should be unconcerned with punching the clock. Rather, we should be

> WE NEED TO BE PASSIONATE ABOUT OUR LOVE FOR GOD AND THE WORLD AROUND US.

concerned 24/7 about the welfare of our flock as well as the lost condition of this world. We need to be passionate about our love for God and the world around us. The psalmist said, *"As the hart panteth after the water brooks, so panteth my soul after thee,*

O God. My soul thirsteth for God, for the living God: when shall I come and appear before God?" (Psalm 42:1–2). That's passion! Are you panting and thirsty for God and the world for which His Son died?

ELEVEN

TWENTY-ONE IDEAS TO BOOST YOUR MISSIONS CONFERENCE

The missions conference should be an event that the entire congregation looks forward to annually—or bi-annually. At Fairfax Baptist Temple, we have always had an annual conference—we call it our Missions Conference Revival—the last week of April, which is the last week of our missions year. I selected a missions year of May through April so that there would be sufficient distance between the time that we present the church budget, which operates on a calendar-year cycle, and the time we present the missions budget. The annual church budget is presented to the congregation the Sunday before Thanksgiving, providing about six months between the two budget events. Doing so, I believe, helps the congregation to view the church operating budget as completely distinct from the missions budget.

After having just one annual missions conference for a few years, the thought came to me that it would be nice to have a missions refresher in the late fall of the year, just before the Christmas giving season. This way, when we presented the congregation with the special Christmas offering list, which predominately identifies projects related to missions and church planting efforts, the joy of hosting some of the missionary-evangelists would be fresh on their minds. Having both the spring and fall conferences helps to keep world evangelism at the forefront of everything we do. Following are some practices we have established to keep our church focused on world evangelism year-round:

1. DISPLAY THE FLAGS

You will probably not be surprised that my first suggestion for boosting your missions conference(s) is to leave your missions flags displayed in the auditorium or another highly visible place year round. Hanging above the doors that exit the auditorium, we have the flags of every country in which we have a missionary evangelist.

As the people leave each service, they have a visual reminder that truly the sun never sets on the ministries supported by Fairfax Baptist Temple. In our former facilities, the flags lined three walls around the auditorium as a reminder that the Great Commission to every local church is to reach people everywhere in the world.

At the time of our actual missions conference, we place additional flags across the back of the platform to represent the nations of the missionary-evangelists present at this conference. We also use the flags for the opening ceremony. From time to time, we appoint teens to carry flags down the main aisle of the auditorium followed by deacons escorting the missionary-evangelists whose country those flags represent as the missions director introduces the family to the congregation. This procession allows everyone to see all the special guests we are honoring.

2. GET THE CHILDREN INVOLVED

A practice that has boosted our main spring conference tremendously is having our Master's Kids Choir (composed of more than eighty first through sixth graders) present an hour-long program on Saturday evening of the conference. The missions-themed program is a great way for the children to be actively involved in the missions conference. It is the last of the four programs that the MKC presents during the choir year and the final program for the sixth graders, providing them with a very special memory of meaningful participation in the missions program. One year, the storyline of MKC Christmas program involved a grandfather's salvation experience. Then during the next missions conference, the storyline followed this grandfather to the mission field where his grandchildren came to visit him. Besides being a terrific way to tie things together, it demonstrated that it is never too late to be involved in missions and highlighted the value of missions trips. By the way, none of our first through sixth graders can drive, so their parents have to attend as well!

3. HAVE LARGE CONFERENCES

Having the largest conference you can afford is a sure way of impacting the minds of the congregation.

We strive to have a good mix of our own veteran missionary-evangelists and others we have not supported before, whether they are new to the field or veterans of many years. It is, of course, a greater undertaking and a significant commitment to have new missionary-evangelists at the conference, because you are taking on a new monthly obligation that will continue until the rapture.

We start scheduling families for the conferences about two years in advance of the date. Doing this allows us to coordinate with the missionary-evangelist's furlough schedule, and it allows the missionary-evangelist an opportunity to save on travel costs by scheduling other churches in our general area. Scheduling ahead is more advantageous to including missionary-evangelists from every continent. The diversity of fields gives the congregation a good sense of world evangelism's global expanse.

A couple of the requirements we ask of the missionary-evangelist are that he bring his entire family with him (except for the children in college) and that he commit to being at the entire program—Wednesday through Sunday nights for the spring conference and Friday through Sunday for the fall conference.

Our conference has a two-fold purpose: first, I desire the missionary-evangelists to bless and edify our church family, and second, I want our church to bless and encourage the missionaries. We train our people to go out of their way to minister to each missionary-evangelist, each wife, and each child while they are with us. For this reason, if the missionary-evangelist or new stateside church planter is unable to bring his whole family or stay through the whole conference, we understand, but we prefer to schedule him for some other time.

4. MAKE ADEQUATE PLANS

A missions conference is not an event you can just add to the schedule. Much planning and work goes into having a successful conference. I suggest that you budget adequately for the annual (or bi-annual) missions conference. Be as generous as you can, and be sure to cover all the expenses, which include a lot of little things that may not amount to much until you total the costs. Depending on your plans for the conference, compute a planning figure to ease you through the budget process. We currently (2010) use $1,200 per family as the guide for the spring conference. We use a slightly smaller number for the fall because it is shorter and we host fewer families. If you plan to have a guest keynote speaker in addition to the missionary-evangelists, be sure to plan for that expense as well. Sometimes we have a keynote speaker and other times we use only our invited missionary-evangelists.

What do we do? We host a dinner for the invited families and the church staff families before the opening night service and a picnic at the pastor's house on Friday afternoon of the conference. We give the wives and children spending money for an organized shopping trip following a special luncheon for the missionaries' wives and our church ladies on Thursday. We buy the men a new suit or an equivalent (such as a nice watch with our church logo) and give each missionary a soulwinner's New Testament and an honorarium/expense check. We also discount items the missionary-evangelists purchase through our bookstore. If you decide to have a keynote speaker, you will probably want to house him at a local hotel rather than with a church family and provide him with transportation while he is in the area if he does not drive to the conference.

5. SUPPORT ALL THE MEN YOU INVITE

I am aware, from talking to missionary-evangelists, that they are invited to some conferences without knowing whether the church will support them. While they are at the conference, the pastor may assemble the men and tell them that out of this group only a few will actually receive support. At other churches, the missionary-evangelists are told that no decision will be made until some weeks or months after the conference. Neither of these is my preference.

We have made it our practice since the founding of our church to plan to support every missionary-evangelist we invite to our church services. At the concluding service on Sunday night, we vote to support every new missionary-evangelist present and increase the support of the others. It is refreshing to the missionary-evangelists not to have to wait weeks or months before finding out about their support. It will be an untold blessing both to the missionary-evangelists and to your people to immediately include them in your missionary-evangelist family.

Inviting only those missionary-evangelists that you intend to support requires a process of prescreening those who are invited. Of course, if the church is new or doesn't have sufficient funds to support new missionary-evangelists, then inform them of your situation ahead of time so that they will have no surprises.

When a missionary-evangelist contacts Fairfax Baptist Temple, there are four basic concerns about which we inquire. First there is the question of his sending church; second, the college he attended; third, his mission board if he has one; and fourth, his philosophy of missions work to include the kind of music he will use. Regarding the sending church, we try to learn as much as we can about it before we inquire too deeply into the man himself. Why? Our philosophy is this: when we are not the sending church, we are joining with his sending church by supporting the missionary-evangelist whom they are sending to replicate their church. If the church is not of like faith and practice, then we cannot in good conscience unite with them. The basic biblical principle of reproducing is that each is to reproduce after its own kind.

If the sending church is of like faith and practice, we then inquire about the man's college and mission board because, knowing the basic stance and philosophies of the various colleges and mission boards, we gain invaluable information about the man. Some of these institutions we cannot support for various reasons, and therefore, we know what line of questioning we would need to use with the candidate.

We make sure that the man shares our missions philosophy (he plans to be actively, personally, and primarily a church planter, not the pastor of a church in a foreign country supported by U.S. missions dollars). Of course, if he is a stateside church planter, our prayer is that he will stay with it and pastor the church for many years. We have found that our questioning must be thorough because sometimes we use the same terminology but have different definitions.

6. HAVE THE MISSIONARIES STAY IN HOMES WITH YOUR FAMILIES

One of the primary reasons for the missions conference is to give the congregation an opportunity to get to know some of God's choicest servants. The church becomes somewhat acquainted within the setting of the church services. However, the best opportunity for a family to really get to know the missionary-evangelist, to catch his burden, to have their hearts made sensitive to world evangelism, is to have the missionary-evangelists stay in their homes. Some of my wife's greatest recollections of missionary-evangelists are sitting around and listening to the missionaries' stories when she was a girl and her parents had missionary-evangelists stay in their home or come over for dinner.

When you place missionaries in homes, it is good to ask them well in advance if they have any pet allergies or special dietary requirements and if they have their own transportation. Be sensitive to the number and ages of the missionary-evangelist's children. Knowing these details, you will be able to provide a housing situation that is comfortable for the host and for the visiting family.

It is also important to make sure the host's home is sufficient for hosting a family. They shouldn't be required to sleep on the top bunk in the children's room or to share a bathroom with the rest of the family!

7. HAVE THE CHURCH FAMILIES PROVIDE MEALS FOR THE MISSIONARIES

Another idea for giving the church family opportunity to meet the missionary-evangelists and to learn firsthand about the various works is to have the congregation host the missionary-evangelists for the evening and Sunday meals. Having the missionary-evangelists dine with other families takes some of the burden and expense off the host families and provides many more opportunities for church families to engage the visiting missionary-evangelists so that they will be able to better pray for them. If the host family prefers, they could also sign up for one or more of the main meals since they may otherwise have very little time with them.

8. CALL YOUR MEETINGS A MISSIONS CONFERENCE REVIVAL

In other words, you should make this the most exciting, most prepared for, and most anticipated event of the year! You and the staff should prepare the congregation spiritually before the event, building up to it in your teaching and preaching so that the hearts of the people are prepared to hear from God through His preachers. If you have two conferences annually, make sure that the weekend of the second conference does not sneak up on everyone. These should be the most important events of the year.

We use the same theme, logos, and booklet design for both conferences. This provides continuity and, frankly, reduces some of the detail work that has to be done. There's nothing wrong with suggesting to the speaker(s) what you would like them to cover (e.g., grace giving, the call to the ministry, the role of young ladies, the needs in various countries, etc.).

9. EARNESTLY PRAY FOR LABORERS

You can boost the effectiveness and excitement of the missions conference by earnestly praying that God will raise up (more) missionary-evangelists from your congregation. This takes an investment of time and emotion. We often admonish our people concerning the blessings of God that *"ye have not, because ye ask not"* (James 4:2). I suggest applying that admonition in a very real way to the missions conference and continuing it throughout the year.

As I have discussed in the earlier pages of this book, it is the responsibility of every church to reproduce. It will not happen if you are not praying to God to make it happen. Remember that God's solution to the lack of workers in the work force is not to worry or complain but to pray. *"Pray ye therefore the Lord of the harvest, that he will send forth laborers into his harvest"* (Matthew 9:38). When was the last time you earnestly prayed for God to raise up more laborers in the church where you minister?

10. SCHEDULE ENOUGH TIME

There are a few different ways to schedule a missions conference. Have your larger missions conference run from Wednesday through Sunday, or even for a full week, Sunday to Sunday. The advantage of ending on Sunday is that you end up with your biggest crowd when you take your new financial commitments. Also, those commitments will be made in hearts that have been sitting under the preaching of God's Word for five days or more. Our shorter fall conference runs Friday night through Sunday. At this conference, we are giving the opportunity for new members to make commitments, and asking others to consider increasing theirs.

During the conference, we give each of the missionary-evangelists an opportunity to show their DVD and explain their work. A staff member pre-screens all of the audiovisual presentations for content and music. We want to make sure their presentation includes church planting and people, not just tourist information. The music must meet our standards, with only a slight allowance for the cultural distinctions of the lesser-developed countries.

11. TEACH GRACE GIVING REGULARLY

I recommend that you teach grace giving every year as a way to boost your missions conference. I have taught grace giving during a missions conference and before a missions conference with, I think, equal effectiveness. Most often, when I am the keynote speaker at a conference, grace giving is one of the topics I preach. Biblical giving is a supernatural act of a renewed heart, and our people need to be reminded of their duty of faithfulness beyond their tithes and offerings.

> BIBLICAL GIVING IS A SUPERNATURAL ACT OF A RENEWED HEART.

Since we started out in the '70s, I have been in many churches and seen different approaches to missions. Some simply give a certain percentage of their general budget to missions. This practice is good, but I don't think it's best. It basically requires no faith of the congregation and very little of the pastor and staff. However, when a church adopts grace giving, which is an annual financial commitment above one's tithes and offerings, people have an opportunity to personally act on their faith in a very real way. I remind us that *"without faith it is impossible to please him"* (Hebrews 11:6).

12. HAVE A LADIES' LUNCHEON

During the spring conference, one of the highlights is a ladies' luncheon. This is open to all the ladies of the church and, of course, to our guests, the missionary-evangelist wives and daughters. During the luncheon the missionary-evangelist wives are given opportunity to tell their favorite stories of life on the mission field. The wives who are on deputation with their husbands may tell of God's care and provision during their travels or share something of interest they gleaned from a survey trip. The pastor's wife might bring a brief devotional. After the luncheon, we take the wives shopping. During this time, the men have lunch together, and then we take them to buy their gift suit or to some other activity.

During the fall conference, we host the ladies for a Saturday brunch. This is for the staff wives, the missionary-evangelist wives, and the home-host wives (which really helps the transportation problem).

13. HAVE A MEN'S BREAKFAST

Saturday morning is a great time to hold a men's breakfast for all married and single men and teen boys. During this activity, you might have a missionary bring a devotional message. We also use this time to allow the men of the church to give a word of testimony about how God is working in their lives. After the breakfast, the single adult group washes the missionary-evangelists' vehicles while the other men go out on door-to-door visitation. This is another opportunity for the men of the church to have some one-on-one time with a missionary-evangelist. When we have an intern ready for ordination, we hold the ordination counsel in place of the visitation, inviting the missionary-evangelists to actively participate with us in examining the candidate.

14. HAVE A CONFERENCE KICK-OFF DINNER

The way we start our two conferences each year is to have a special welcome dinner before the conference for all the missionaries and their families with the purpose of providing a relaxing time in which my staff and I meet and greet the invited guests. Our people prepare a fabulous meal, using real silverware and dishes! All the details are thought out, down to special little name cards on the tables.

Pastor, if you have no staff, you could host this meal at your home (if your wife is up to it), or perhaps someone else could prepare the meal and serve it at the church (if you have church facilities), or you could have it catered.

After dinner, we give the missionary-evangelists a welcome packet (including the agenda of preaching/teaching times, the home at which they will be staying, the meal schedule for the week), and I share with them the expectations for the conference.

I use this forum to reiterate to the missionary-evangelists our philosophy of missions—church planting. Then I tell them to relax and enjoy the conference! I let them know that they are not on trial or under scrutiny. Rather, we are looking for them to join us in the mammoth task of evangelizing the world. We want colaborers!

Regarding their accommodations, I ask them not to be critical if something is amiss in the home in which they are staying or dining (these families may be new converts). I encourage them to help the family in a kind, gentle, and loving way, seeking to be a blessing.

To be equitable, I ask them not to make any financial pleas at any time, even when they present their work. It would be unfair if some presented needs (they all have needs) and others didn't. I tell our missionaries to let us know their particular needs so that we can consider helping them.

15. HAVE THE MISSIONARIES IN YOUR ACADEMY CLASSES

If you have a church school, utilize the missionary-evangelists and their families during the school day. We schedule the missionary-evangelists to visit classes in all the grades. We ask the missionary-evangelists to talk to the students about the field, especially their contact with people the same ages as the students. By the way, being in attendance at all of the services is a requirement in our Bible classes. We urge the students who are not members of Fairfax Baptist Temple to attend on the nights when there is no service in their home church.

While the missionary-evangelists are on campus, we keep a hospitality room open where they can relax when they are not assigned to be in a certain place.

16. ENCOURAGE THE CHILDREN TO HAVE THEIR BIBLES SIGNED

In the church school, during the midweek children's program and in the children's church, encourage the young people to get the missionary-evangelists to sign their Bibles. In the missions booklet, we include a place for the missionary-evangelists to sign their name and record their life's verse. We challenge the children to get the signatures of all of the missionary-evangelists during the conference. In fact, this is a nice thing for the adults to do as well. When they see that name in their Bibles, they will remember a face and pray for them (I hope).

17. GIVE EACH MISSIONARY AN OPPORTUNITY TO SHARE HIS BURDEN

It is important that each of the missionary-evangelists has an opportunity to present his work to the church. Our church has used a variety of venues for the visual presentations. We have some in the services. Sometimes we have break-out rooms on a Saturday evening so that the church people can move from room to room to hear the presentations. One year, the missions booklet was designed like a passport, and we encouraged the congregation to get their passport "stamped" (signed) as they visited each country. We also have the missionary-evangelist's displays set up in the lobby throughout the conference. They stand near their displays before and after the services to talk with people as they walk by.

18. USE THE MUSICAL TALENT OF THE MISSIONARIES

Some of the missionary-evangelists are skilled musicians. It is a good boost to the missions conference when you utilize the missionary-evangelists for special music, the offertory, and so forth. This is also a good way to involve the missionary-evangelists' children. It is wise to have a staff member listen to the music before the service to make sure their selections comply with the music standards.

19. HAVE MISSIONARY TESTIMONIES

In addition to showing the missionary-evangelists' presentations, have one or more of the missionary-evangelists give a testimony. One of the things that I encourage the men to discuss is how they recognized God's call and how God directed them to their specific place of service. You may want to have the missionary-evangelists' wives participate with their husbands in the testimony. If you do this, tell each husband that the majority of the time should be his. We have found it best to let the missionaries know in advance their approximate time limit so that we do not lose control of the length of the service.

20. GIVE GIFTS TO THE MISSIONARIES

Giving the missionaries gifts is a unique and exciting conference closer. We ask the missionary-evangelists ahead of time to send us a list of five to ten things—within the price range of $50–$100—that they either need or simply want. Sometimes we get requests for things like a new computer, printer, set of tires, etc. I think some of them have been overseas too long and have forgotten what things actually cost! We try to distribute this list at least a couple of months prior to the conference to give our people plenty of time to sign up and purchase the gifts.

If you have more "givers" than you have gift requests, simply suggest that they purchase a Wal-Mart, restaurant (national chains like McDonald's), gas, or generic gift card (Visa, American Express) to give as gifts.

The gifts are all wrapped and presented at the closing service on Sunday night. You cannot imagine the impact this has on the missionary-evangelists and on those giving the gifts.

21. MAKE THE CLOSING SERVICE SPECIAL

The first thing we do at the close of the last service is to have all the missionary-evangelists and their families come to the platform and give each of the men a New Testament and an honorarium. The pastor then recommends that we take on the new missionary-evangelists for support and increase the veteran missionary-evangelists' support. Next we have our people come forward and present the gifts. After this, we tell our people to give the missionary-evangelists a Fairfax Baptist Temple (name of your church) "thank you." When the pastor says that, we all rise and give them a standing ovation, not to feed their flesh, but to let them know that we love them and honor them for their labor of love.

I said at the first and I repeat now, the missions conference should be an event excitedly anticipated by the entire congregation!

CONCLUSION

Whether you are a pastor seeking to send out men to plant churches, or a man that is called of God to be a church planter, or just an interested Christian, I hope that you have found something of value in exchange for the time you spent reading this book. There is one final thought that I want to share with you. Regardless of how well you follow the principles of this book, if you leave prayer and the power of God out of it you *will not* be successful in your labors. Church planting is a spiritual work that can only be accomplished by Spirit-led and Spirit-filled men. You cannot be Spirit-led if you are not regularly in communication with the God whose church you are seeking to help build.

As a missionary-evangelist or pastor-teacher you are God's gift to the church. As a gift from God, you are to be a part of the description set out in James 1:17: *"Every good gift and every perfect gift is from above, and cometh down from the Father of lights, with whom is no variableness, neither shadow of turning."* *Good* in the sense of beneficial to the church, and *perfect* in the sense of being complete in your mental, moral and spiritual character. You must be a student of the Word of God. Upon asking him for a word of advice, Dr. Charles Woodbridge gave me a three word mission statement as I was about to start Fairfax Baptist Temple: Master the Book! I am still working to achieve that mission, and I would highly recommend every man of God do the same.

As a missionary-evangelist or church planter you will be pulled in a thousand directions at once. You need to ensure that you have your time of personal devotion and prayer at the beginning of each day. This means you will have to learn to be an early riser and a disciplined man. Maintaining your personal walk with God will be the most important thing you do each day. You have to care for your wife and family. (As a sidebar, please underscore that last sentence. Remember, your wife and family are also the ministry, and one in which you will have to give an account. Never discount time with them because you are so involved "in the ministry." That may sound spiritual but shows a complete lack of understanding regarding one's biblical responsibility to his family.) This means you have to be an able scheduler and willing to be jealous of family time. You need to be out knocking on doors. You need to be visiting people that visit your church and available to counsel your own. You need to prepare three sermons and a Sunday school lesson each and every week. Did you get tired just reading through this list?

This will be your life for the years ahead of you. What I hope is obvious is that if you try to do this work in your own strength you will very likely not succeed, at least not from a spiritual or eternal perspective. Pray!

One of the things that you should be praying about most fervently is that God would send to you a colaborer. You need the strength that comes from sharing the work with someone to whom you can grow close. I was blessed to have a friend come to the very first meeting held in my apartment who then stayed with me for many years. As I read the Gospels, Acts, and the epistles the one constant is that the men that were sent out went as a team. Ecclesiastes 4:9 is exactly right when we read *"Two are better than one; because they have a good reward for their labour."*

If you have not yet started the journey, take advantage of the time to prepare sermons; completely or in substantial outline form. This will be a tremendous advantage as you try to be all things to all people. You know what the special days are, and when they come: Thanksgiving, Christmas, Mother's Day, Father's Day, Independence Day, and Easter. If you have these sermons prepared then the days are less likely to sneak up on you. Keep in mind that one of the hardest exercises in good homiletics is thinking of stimulating and appropriate illustrations to shed light on the truths you are seeking to communicate.

This should be obvious, but prepare your *own* sermons. The internet is a wonderful tool and there is a plethora of sermon-helps and study-helps sites, but these tools should be used only in addition to what God is doing in your heart and through your own devotional walk with Him. As you read your Bible, take a second to jot down key words, phrases or thoughts with the reference. As you develop your list, you can place the ideas in various categories. I always put an asterisk in the margin by any verse that God used to speak to my own heart, knowing He could do the same for others. If you do this faithfully then you will never be at a loss for a sermon idea. Another way to accomplish this is to have in mind a few topics that you know already that you want to teach to your people. Perhaps you want to talk about soulwinning or prayer or sanctification. As you read, jot down references or verses that touch on the topic. This will cut down on your preparation time as the Spirit guides your thoughts concerning the Word He superintends. Of course you also want to preach through books of the Bible, and in my opinion the best one to start with is the Gospel of John, which is designed to build up people's faith.

Finally, do not neglect to continue to seek after and develop God's passion for world evangelism. God cares about *all* people on planet earth, and it is our responsibility as pastors and leaders in the church to keep this perspective before us at all times. God designed church planting to be the means to carry out His work of reaching a world for Himself. Perhaps it has been a while since you or your church has been engaged directly in church planting. There is no time like the present to commit/recommit to His purpose and cause. I have always believed that if we take care of God's business (world evangelism), He will take care of ours!

> *Now unto him that is able to do exceeding abundantly*
> *above all that we ask or think, according to the power*
> *that worketh in us, Unto him be glory in the church*

by Christ Jesus throughout all ages, world without end. Amen.—EPHESIANS 3:20–21

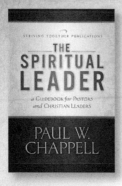

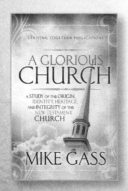

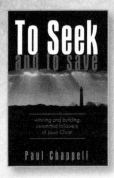
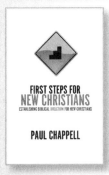

Visit us online

strivingtogether.com

wcbc.edu